A Calling Of Angels

— Bridging Two Worlds —

Frances Hollis-Powles

A Calling Of Angels
— *Bridging Two Worlds* —

ISBN 0-9535210-7-9
ISBN 978-0-9535210-7-4

Front cover photograph of Frances by Ceawyn Holland

Printed in the UK
Published by R.A. Associates
For information - mail@whitefeather.org.uk

Contents

A Calling Of Angels

Prelude

From the kitchen, I sensed something was in the living room. Something, that was trying to attract my attention. Very quietly I slid the joint of meat back into the oven. Picking up the meat fork, while attempting to ignore my pounding heart and the twists in my stomach, I crept out of the kitchen. Fork at the ready to spear the intruder, I plucked up the courage to enter the room.

An eerie silence filled the space. Chills wrapped themselves around me. The air was still as if time had stopped. I could hear my breathing as if high decibels rattled aloud within my body.

The room became so cold; I was chilled to the bone. Suddenly and alarmingly a vast spray of colours filled the room. So immediate, as if they had been there all the time.

Within it's centre, in a shower of white, silver, and pale blue lights stood a man dressed in a plain pale suit. No wings, or halo but every inch an Angel, shining his love toward me. My fears melted away as I seemed to recognise him. I sensed we'd known each other somewhere before this moment. Sometime from a time that echo's the distant past.

"You have been called to Mediumship" He spoke softly with no audible tone. "We will serve humanity together, the Realms of Spirit and you. To embrace, both sides of the veil."

Briefly, he mentioned a local church, and the name of the President. "At this church you will endeavour to help others. You will be taught by us, in our World to help people understand the Spirit Realms, adding "Your work will change over the years ahead of you and one thing that must be clearly stated, everyone will benefit who comes in contact with you."

As he completed his conversation with me, the colours began to fade inward. I could "Hear" his Voice, and always have, when I'm ready to serve.

Chapter One
A calling of angels

As a born spiritual medium, I've always felt closer to the Angels than earth people. I feel a warm glow that I've been lucky enough to be chosen by those in the Angel realms to smooth the connection between earth and those angels of the light. Just a delicate touch from me allows these angels to blend love with sincerity as they pass on information full of harmony and wisdom.

As a British Spiritual Medium, I was always so aware of grief in others. It became vital to fulfil my life's pathway, which I learnt early on was to help others who do not have the gift of communication.

It all began in the outside loo in the early '50s when I was about 5 years old. It was quite usual then for terraced houses to have outside toilets. You were very posh if you had a bathroom installed in the house. Our outside toilet was pretty basic, a plain ordinary door with a barrel opening and bar for privacy. Often I'd be occupying the loo and singing to myself, when the door would seem to fade away and be replaced by a pale white cloud. Looking back, I suppose it was just like watching a television screen, although I certainly didn't know what television looked like as it was not as available then as it is today. I was convinced that invisible wires had attached themselves to the inside of my head which passed on all the news. Everything I saw seemed interesting and colourful as time after time I was shown news of future events, some as far off as fifteen years or so in the future, while a voice explained the startling visions which I was too young to understand. Thrilled, I often received important news before my parents heard it announced over the wireless. I can remember running back indoors, with all sorts of extraordinary titbits tumbling out of my mouth.

'There were three gentlemen playing guitars, and one playing a big drum,' I announced excitedly one day. 'They comb their hair straight down, not a bit like Tony Curtis. The drum had a large creepy-crawly like a beetle on the front. And they're going to be famous one day.' I ran out of breath.

'Oho yes!' replied an understanding mother, winking at my father. 'They sound bloody awful,' he grunted.

I expect they did. After all, in the early '50s, all singing groups modelled their hair styles on one film star or another and didn't start calling themselves after inanimate objects until the famous Beatles arrived, in the early Sixties.

Another time, the pictures showed me adult women wearing short skirts. I asked if these skirts would be as short as tennis skirts, which were then just above the knees.

'No!' said the gentle voice. 'Much shorter.' I blushed and ran out of the loo, refusing to listen to any more rude talk. That was for grown-ups.

The voice made me feel secure and cared for. I never felt threatened or frightened by it, just annoyed sometimes. Why did I have to listen to this each time I used the loo? It didn't happen when I used any other toilet, and no one else mentioned the voice in our toilet. It was all very perplexing.

When I was seven, the pattern changed. I'd done the unforgivable. I'd answered back my normally- placid parents and after a terrible telling-off, been sent to my room in floods of tears.

'Where are you? Don't leave me, I need you so much,' I appealed to the voices I'd always sent packing before. My voice trailing off, I buried my tear-stained face in the snowy white pillowcase, feeling so sad. Suddenly I felt an overwhelming urge to look up towards the window. Wiping my tears away with my cardigan sleeve, I stared in disbelief at the window. Something was stirring within it. To my thrilled amazement, a ball of light entered my bedroom, spraying white, silver and blue rays everywhere. Within the breathtaking light was a comforting voice which sounded as if it belonged to a cultured Englishman. I instinctively knew I was in the company of a spiritual friend, one I had known long before I'd arrived on the earth.

'Can I come back home?' I pleaded.

'No, little one, your life has not yet begun.' His voice seemed to smile, his honey brown tones making me feel so very loved and valued. I searched the light for a face or a body but there was only the voice. 'You have a great deal to do in this lifetime and many tasks to fulfil.' His gentle voice calmed me as he explained my pathway. 'We will be close to you, never fear, we are only a prayer away.'

His voice trailed off leaving me engulfed in a blanket of healing love, the likes of which I had never before or since known. Then the light slowly melted into tiny pockets of air, leaving the bedroom empty.

'It's not fair! It just isn't fair! No one wants me,' I screamed, racing desperately to the window. That was it. Rejected by 'them' as well. The world was against me, BOTH worlds. So the spirit realms and I were not talking, well, I wasn't anyway.

It was a while before I would accept any more information after that and so the spirit realms withdrew. I finally made contact again by calling them. I was then given information which I hope will never come true. I was told that future generations would look upon household taps as a novelty of the past, as all drinking water would be purchased at huge shops which I can only assume must be supermarkets. At the time, we had never heard of supermarkets, everybody shopped at corner stores.

I am often asked how I began as a working medium. Was I a child medium? Did I 'see' other little spirit children and play with them? My answer is always the same. I didn't have small spirit friends to talk and play with. The only communicators were young adults who were always very well spoken. They didn't constantly speak to me or appear daily, or for that matter regularly at all. When they did appear, I usually told them to get lost or shut up. They were too old to play with me. They were more like older brothers and sisters, spending a few short minutes with a little sister before dashing off to do something far more grown-up. I didn't know I was different, I thought everyone had 'communicators'. Everyone has seen or heard a ghost, haven't they? Knowing what I do now, I'm surprised anyone chose to stay around me long enough to become my spirit guide.

I would have to go back to the womb to describe how it all really started. My mother had lost her father exactly one year before my arrival into this world. While she was pregnant with me, my mother experienced a visitation from her father three mornings in a row, accompanied by what appeared to be Roman soldiers. He had come to ask her and my father to take care of Mum's mother, now that she was alone in the world. When my mother carried my brother she did not have any such experiences, that was the only one! I once had a comical story to explain why I became a medium. I was walking around the spirit world one day, when I happened to see a gathering of people. Being extremely nosy, I drew closer to find out what was happening. A tall gentleman, talking to the group, pointed to me.

'Come on, Frances,' he said, waving me towards a tunnel. I was a little hard of hearing, so I didn't realise that what he'd really said was, 'Who fancies their chances?' Too late. I had gone through the tunnel, missing the overhead sign which read 'Mediums and healers for earth'. So it was an accident, not a gift, that I am a medium.

My childhood was as normal as anyone else's, despite all the wacky instances which I now realise were moulding me in my youth for mediumship later in life. My loving parents, Patrick and Lorna, have always been very special to me, showing tremendous patience and always full of love and cuddles for my brother Steven and me. We learnt early in life to see the best in everyone which meant we could see the best in ourselves.

My father came from North Wales while my mother has always lived in Newport South Wales. My father grew up in the Catholic faith while Mum was Church of England. This by fairness made me the same faith as my mother and brother Steven followed the Catholic side. But I spent more time in the Catholic faith than anywhere else, that is, until I found other churches. They seemed to me to be a rich collection of churches, all coming from different directions but still working toward the same goal. The Almighty God. I can recall as a child telling my mother that the sky was our church, the altar is the heart beating inside us, that is where we find our god. Go to it regularly, and you will find your god. I was very young but Mum didn't laugh at me. She always listened to what I said, then gave her opinion which was always fair.

Steven and I are so lucky that our parents chose us for their children before we were born. This is quite common. When group souls need to work out a plan which cannot be dealt with before birth, they form a partnership at some stage of their lives to help or assist in another karma or destiny.

Since I become involved with this work, my father has chosen to become involved also. His involvement is with spiritual healing, which he found rewarding and gratifying.

Over the years that followed the spirit visit when I was seven, strange 'happenings' took place which I had no control over. Because I'd built up a sort of fog which became a barrier to 'them', I wasn't given any explanations for these 'happenings'. As I grew older, boyfriends became far more important than my voices of childhood. Looking back, I can see the spirits were often close to me during the years of health problems, childbirth, divorce and subsequent remarriage. But they left me alone until I had more experience of life. After all, how could I know another's pain or grief, understand just how many levels of depression a person can sink to, unless I'd been there? All these emotions lay in my path so I could understand them when I started to help others.

I was pregnant with my first child when a 'voice' of golden brown tones spoke to me quite unexpectedly.

'Your true husband is a soldier and you will meet him one day soon.' You could have knocked me over with a baby's rattle. Here I was, large as life, carrying my husband's baby, our first child, and I was hearing all this rubbish from the spirit realms.

'Well,' I answered loudly, 'You got that one wrong, didn't you?' I was quite happy, we were looking forward to spending our lives together. We'd met when children, living not far from one another, got engaged when I was sixteen and married at eighteen. How wrong the spirit voices were.

It was after we'd had our second child that my husband informed me that he'd met someone else and wanted a divorce. So the spirit realms had been right! Only one thing was wrong. I didn't want anybody else, I could not trust any man long enough to settle. Whether he was a soldier or tramp, I did not want anything to do with men!

For two years the children and I lived with my parents, who looked after the two little ones during the day so I could work. My life was work, home, bed. My only friend was Christine. One day she showed me photos of her little one's Christening. We laughed at the arms holding the baby. They were heavily tattooed and were all you could see, as the rest of the man, who was the baby's godfather, would not fit in the photo.

Unexpectedly after work one evening, Christine dropped into my parents' home. Her husband had offered to baby-sit so she could go out for the night.

'And your mother's baby-sitting for you,' exclaimed an excited Chris, 'Get your glad rags on. We're going up town for the night.'

'But I don't drink,' I stuttered.

'You will tonight, girl,' replied my wicked friend. I was very nervous, afraid of a scene if we bumped into my soon to be ex-husband, so I sent Christine in first to see if the pub was safe. I waited and waited but she didn't return so I had to go in and find her. She was talking to two men at the bar. They called me over to join them but when I spotted that one looked like a forty-year-old tattooed gorilla, it took a lot from me to sit with them and get comfortable. As it turned out, we had a great night. The gorilla, who was called Keith, had just left the army after nine years. He plagued me to see him again which I did. In fact, a year after that, we got married in a small wedding. Our other two children came very quickly after that, a boy, then a girl. That was over thirty-seven years ago. We celebrated many wedding anniversaries, my soldier and me. I have often thought of the voices all those years ago while I was pregnant with my first baby. She is nearly thirty-five now. I did not believe what they said at that time but they were correct all the same. I'm glad they were. But I won't tell my gorilla that.

When Keith and I first got married we lived in a little council house. We returned from a week's holiday to be greeted by some very concerned neighbours. Apparently our bedroom curtains had been pushed back and forth, making everyone think we had burglars or dare I mention it, a ghost? They were convinced it was the latter - everyone likes to think they've spotted a ghost, don't they? They suggested we inspected the house very carefully. Once inside, I dashed for the food cupboard. arguing if it was burglars they would have eaten us out of house and home. The cupboards were still half full, as we had left them. Keith had raced upstairs straightaway, hoping to catch the culprits red-handed but the bedrooms were empty. So we concluded whoever was playing with the bedroom curtains could stay. Maybe they'd warn off prospective burglars - not many thieves will break into a house with a ghost patrolling each room - and ghosts would not eat and drink us out of everything. Money was tight then.

The spirits left me alone for years to learn from my life experiences but even then, I still retained an interest in the paranormal. I concentrated on bringing up my family before anything else but even then, in my quieter hours, I'd play with cards or sand divining. When I mentioned to Keith that I was able to see and hear people who were invisible, he asked me to tell his fortune, which is the usual response. I told him I couldn't do it, then I went into great depth about what I could do.

It was Keith who was responsible for my first forays into working with the public. I'd mentioned something about wanting a crystal ball. One Christmas Eve, we were sitting down enjoying some peace and quiet after the children had eventually gone to bed. I could see my present from Keith was sitting under the tree. It was large, square and very heavy. Suddenly I could see through the wrapping paper and into the box. It was a crystal ball. I equally suddenly knew that I didn't want or need it. The following morning, I tried to show my delight when I opened it. He was so pleased I liked it but I knew deep inside that this wasn't the way forward for me. Still, maybe it was worth a try.

My eldest daughter Julie came home from work one day to tell me how she had been discussing me with a colleague. My heart missed a beat as she confessed she had blurted out to this colleague that I was a fortune-teller. At long last I was recognised as someone I had always admired. Julie wanted to know if I could possibly go to this lady's home and give her a reading? My coat was on my shoulders, and, as I searched for my handbag, I explained that tea would be late. Julie stared open mouthed as I ignored cries of 'I'm starving' from my four children.

'Mum, what are you doing?' screeched Julie. 'You'll have to make an appointment to see her. You can't go now. She'll be cooking her family's meal and we'd like ours too.' Meekly I pulled my coat off, trying hard to laugh it off.

'Of course you all want to eat, I was only testing,' I fibbed. My enthusiasms nearly got me in dire straits with four hungry children. Never again. Family must always come first.

It took seven long days before my first client contacted me. At long last she did. I was so excited I could have burst. I hugged myself with glee all day, each time I thought of that evening. What's more, I was even getting paid for it, the princely sum of £2.00.

I'll never forget the excitement of that first evening. I became so engrossed with what lay ahead that, as I walked, the carrier bag holding my large crystal ball hung heavily in my hands. I had by now decided I loved the ball, as it seemed to have opened the way to such an exciting new chapter in my life. Filled with exuberance, I gently swung the bag back and forth. Suddenly back it came, crashing into my shinbone and leaving me hopping about.

I pushed the bag away quickly. The weight of the contents created more swing than I had actually given it. Suddenly I heard a tremendous thud as the handle of the bag gave way. My beloved crystal ball rolled away in front of me, with me chasing it at great speed. But however I tried, I couldn't catch it up. Over and over it rolled inside the bag. It seemed to possess a mind of its own, bouncing over anything in its path. Nothing slowed it down. It shot over stones and flattened discarded cans. Twice I almost caught it up, but again it gained speed. Obviously a streetwise crystal ball which didn't want to get damaged, it only came to rest when a car turned the corner onto its path.

Eventually I reached my first client and the sitting began. I tried to remember all the little tricks I'd learnt about keeping people's interest. Begin with a big sigh, then a puzzled glance, swallow hard and start slowly. When at a couple of points in the reading, I wasn't sure what to say next, I just said whatever came into my head. That would do it, I guessed. I would have added something about wearing red to attract luck but these voices kept echoing in my head and interfering with the reading. The client seemed delighted with everything I told her and pushed the money into my hand. I stared at it in disbelief. I was doing something I loved and getting paid for it.

No-one was more shocked than I was when Julie came home the next day with a message from my client that everything I had said that evening had turned out to be right on the button.

This was wonderful, there would be no stopping me now. All I had to do was a find a way to stop the 'voices' telling me what to say. That may be a little harder. Even so, I thought, 'they' did help quite a lot of the time. So, as their payment should be half the amount, I put £1.00 in a charity box and £1.00 in my pocket.

Word soon got out that a fortune-teller was paying home visits and didn't charge very much. The biggest bugbear was lugging my crystal ball everywhere I went. So I chose instead to work with the cards again. But I found these bothersome and spent more time looking my client straight in the eye than glancing at the cards, which actually I didn't have a clue how to read. More and more I worked with my senses or passed on what the voices urged me to say. I was a medium, but I didn't have a clue that I was. I suppose that was the start of a more active relationship with the spirit realms but I had so much still to learn.

Always wanting to please me, Keith bought me anything I needed and drove me everywhere, even though he remained inside the car for up to two hours at a stretch while I dealt with my work. But I never wanted him to be involved in my work and I tried very hard not to discuss it with him. I always felt that if he held views that I was not interested in, then I'd be so bored if he discussed them with me. So instead, I talked in volumes to anyone else who would listen, then, when I felt competent enough, I went looking for sympathetic victims to try out my newfound gifts. There was always someone ready to test me. Unknown to me then, this was opening up my psychic eye even more to the spirit people.

Although my husband Keith has never ventured into my other worlds, it has not prevented him from keeping me firmly on the ground, instead of carrying on like a 'prima donna'. However, if I should need help in any way, he has always been a tower of strength and often a theory he may suggest can be so interesting. I would like to volunteer a little philosophy about aliens, suggested by my husband. I think it's worth a mention in this book. Much has been said of these wandering souls. If you think for a moment about the world and its cohabitants, have you ever thought that not one person is perfect in every way? Each one of us has a problem, if not health then social or financial. Think if you would how many colours, races and standards we are currently aware of. Could we all be sent here from another world where, perhaps because we had wronged another, we are put on a colony until we have served our time? Every now and again we are visited by these aliens as some sort of warder checking on how we are doing. Just a thought which begins to make some sense to me.

The spirit messengers waited until I was 28 years of age, and married with four children, with just a little more understanding of emotions and life itself, before they made spectacular contact again. By then it seemed I had passed a test of endurance. Twenty-five years ago my son, Martin who was 12 suffered multiple injuries in an accident and was on a life support machine in the University Hospital, Cardiff. I knew I was losing him but the specialists made me go home to sleep. I went to my mother-in-law's first but was too emotional to see people so I sat on a bench outside. I pleaded and begged for help, promising the spirit world that if they saved Martin, I would work with them in whatever way they wanted. The result was a remarkable Sunday morning visit to my living room, a soul that chose to gently engulf me with Spiritual knowledge.

Unspoken words passed between our minds. I fully understood and appreciated each explanation of my future life, as a Medium.

When the spirit had faded and the room was empty once more, I just stared at the place where he'd been, then dashed for the phone directory to look up the letter P for priest. Did you know they're not listed? I thought of running to the local church, then changed my mind. How would I explain I had a GHOST in my house? It's not the same as screaming 'Help! There's a mouse in my house.' They'd have thought I was crackers, and anyway, I reasoned, they were probably in the middle of a service. So I did the next best thing, I phoned my parents although I felt that, at this stage, they only needed to know a veiled version of what had happened. Anything more would have thrown them both into hysteria and resulted in dire warnings of how dangerous it was to tamper with things best left alone. No, for now a brief summary of events would have to suffice.

After that, I had to do a bit of sleuthing, the paranormal kind.

Chapter Two

Here we go!

My first step was to rope my brother in, without telling him too much. Steven kept probing deeper into why I needed to bother with these people. In the end, I just shrugged my shoulders, insisted that I needed to go to this Spiritualist Church, and begged him to come with me. He eventually agreed though he was less happy about not telling our parents what we were about to do. I pleaded with him to find out what he could about this Spiritualist church and he quickly came back with all the information. The church was open most evenings and of course on Sundays. I squeezed my hands in excitement as my heart pounded with a mixture of happiness and caution. I was so confused, but I didn't care, didn't give a hoot. Steven and I were like two little kids again on one of our adventures, only this time we weren't children, and there was a silly feeling that we were being watched by eyes unseen.

Getting through that week was awful, it dragged on, more like a year than a week. Thoughts raced through my mind. It was as if a door had opened to my childhood. All sorts of things started making sense. I remembered the talks I'd had with teenagers in the spirit body. They'd given me all sorts of advice, always brief and often funny, the kind older brothers would give a little sister. I'd enjoyed those episodes until other things turned my head. Now it seemed that all I'd learnt in childhood from my visitors was about to unfold once again, only this time I was mature enough to accept the information. But right now I just needed to investigate The Calling from the spirit worlds and decide whether I would answer it. What on earth did they want that I had?

At that point, I didn't know I had any abilities which would be useful to anyone. I didn't think they'd chosen the right person. I wasn't particularly religious, I've just searched for my rightful path like anyone else, entering countless churches looking for something I couldn't describe. But I didn't see

see that as doing anything special. I recalled telling my mother that the sky is the roof of the people's church and the heart is the altar. I still believed that but I didn't think that entitled an angel to come calling. Oh well, you just don't know who's going to drop in these days, do you?

Eventually, Sunday came. I couldn't contain myself any longer and excitedly told Keith, Steven and my parents what had happened. Father was dead set against my visiting any Spiritualist church and suggested my Ghost needed his Priest instead. He quoted perilous warnings, enough to frighten anyone. That advice wasn't what I needed to hear. But he did make me sit up, listen and think. So when the time arrived to leave for the church, I was excited, shaking with nervous apprehension at what lay ahead, yet with Father's warnings echoing in my ears.

I was so eager to find out if what I'd been told was true. Steven was far more cautious than I, and gave strict instructions that, if anything bizarre should happen, we were both to march straight out and never mention the subject again. I nodded my head, full of anticipation at what lay ahead. These people could have swung from the light fittings and I wouldn't have cared. I knew this was what I had been searching for, or at least, what my heart and soul had longed for, within the quieter hours of my life.

The Spiritualist church was only a twenty-minute walk from my home. The entrance was dark against the warm evening light. Steven and I went down to the basement, as instructed, and there in front of us we found the door we'd been told about. Gingerly we pushed it open onto a staircase which descended into pitch black. It frightened me witless. At the bottom, my fumbling hand found another door and then a handle. Turning this handle, we were relieved to find ourselves in a brightly lit room. A well-dressed gentleman met us, asking us to be very quiet, as the medium had started her presentation to the congregation. A few people turned around briefly but they were far more interested in what was going on in front of them. Steve and I fumbled around for chairs, too busy listening and watching the proceedings to look where we were walking. Two smiling gentlemen placed a couple of chairs at the end of a row for us.

I gripped my handbag tightly in my lap. Suddenly I heard ringing out a familiar hymn, 'Gracious Spirit of Thy Goodness', though to this day, I still don't know why it was familiar or where I'd heard it before. Once the hymn had finished, the medium stood up again. Smiling at the crowd, she spoke to several people, giving them messages she said were passed to her from spirit people standing alongside her. I wondered if she meant the Chinese Mandarins or the Indian Chiefs, though I found it hard to believe that many people in the audience could have such exotic looking relations. I guessed she must mean the people dressed in more ordinary clothes, including some women in long black dresses of a type worn by Welsh women of preceding generations. I was surprised at the number of children running around, and jumped in shock when a couple of dogs appeared out of nowhere, barking and playing with the children. Strangely, no one around me seemed to react to the noise and the fun, even though the colourful sprays of light which surrounded the stage provided such a spectacle. Everyone around the medium seemed to be filled with love for and knowledge of the people in the congregation. Even I could feel the warmth radiating from the carnival of colour parading before our eyes. Yet the congregation seemed oblivious to it all. I found this extraordinary. Why on earth didn't these people acknowledge the forms around the medium? I tried to concentrate on the medium, as again she gave messages to recipients in the crowd, messages I could see her being given by these colourful people who'd lean over her shoulder.

My emotions were building up, I sensed something positive ahead of me. The excitement built quickly, my heart beat faster, confidence filled every inch of my being. Something wonderful and strange was happening in my life but I felt as if it had always been there, like a second skin.

I nudged Steven.

'I can do that,' I whispered confidently.

'Don't be daft. You can't act like that.'

'She's not acting,' I protested, 'She's describing those people around her.'

My brother stared at me.

'I think it's time we got you home,' he said sternly. Why are brothers so bossy, even when you're having fun? But the service seemed to be ending anyway and I didn't want to argue, I might have needed Steve again, so I agreed lamely and got up out of my seat, thinking how much I had 'seen' and enjoyed that evening. I felt completely at home and relaxed and I wanted more of that.

'May I speak to you?' The medium's soothing voice behind made me jump. 'I'm sorry to bother you. I don't normally keep on after a service but you see, a gentleman from the spirit world wishes to be heard.'

I nodded my head.

'The gentleman would like to tell you that he's here to guide you into spiritual matters, so that one day you will also do what I have done tonight.' Her face beamed, while my hair nearly stood on end. At the side of the lady, in a spirit body as large as life itself was the same man who'd been in my living room the previous weekend.

'He does get around,' I stammered under my breath. She didn't need to tell me what he was saying. She could obviously only hear him but I could see him quite clearly and hear what he was saying for myself.

My brother became very interested in what the medium had said and proceeded to question me all the way home.

'How did you know before she did, that you would do the same as her?' he quizzed.

'That's for me to know and you to ask your guide,' I teased laughing. That only succeeded in making him prod me more. But I didn't have a clue about the answers at that stage in my life.

I couldn't stop myself thinking about the spirit guide's words. I began asking myself if I was going ever so slightly around the twist. I kept going to the church each week and soon my dad came with me, to investigate the claims. Over the next month we found the people kind and pleasant, so when they held a student mediums' night, Dad and I went along to give support.

Two of the mediums sat either side of the chairwomen, and the service opened with some lovely hymns. When the time came for the communication with the spirit realms, nothing happened. So we sang another hymn. Still nothing. But by now, I could hear voices clearly in my ear.

'Go on,' they advised, 'We'll help you. We won't let you down.' I began to get very uncomfortable in my seat, squirming constantly.

'What on earth's the matter, Frances?' hissed my father. 'Anyone would think you had fleas.' My elbows started to shake, then my shoulders. Father kept asking me if I was all right. People looked round to see why Dad and I were making so much noise. Still the voices in my ear edged me on, not aggressively, but instilling in me the confidence to try. Well, I decided, standing up, if I was going to make a fool of myself, let it be a big one.

'Ladies and gentlemen, most mediums have gentle voices in their ear that, after a reasonable time, say they are fitted to platform work. I'm hearing encouraging voices practically nagging me to stand and deliver messages from the world of the spirit. All I ask is that you bear with me and be patient. This is my first time, and I have to wait for my instructions.'

If it wasn't so serious I think I would have burst into laughter, yet I felt perfectly normal and knew that once I had started, 'they' would help. It seemed I was ready, and I progressed intuitively. I waited for my prompt from the spirit world. They knew what they were doing, which was more than I did. I moved to about seven people telling them what the voices told me to say. Then the voices gently advised me to stop, thank the congregation, and sit down. People began patting me on the back and congratulating me.

Suddenly, reaction hit and I began to shake. I grabbed Dad's hand and rushed outside.

'It's only nerves, love,' Dad maintained, 'You were great. I'm proud of you, my girl. Now let's get home and tell your mum. Six weeks and you stood in front of all those people, it was marvellous.'
I turned and looked him in the face.

'No, not just me, I had help you wouldn't think existed. They're so beautiful and so caring, and they only want to help everyone see and hear their own loved ones. They're using me to get the messages across. I've only just begun, there's such a lot of work to do, to get people ready for those who will come in the future. We're only paving the way.'

The first thing I had to do was find out my spiritual friend's name. I wasn't going to make any moves until I knew that, however long it took. The answer came quickly - 'Tudor Anderson'. He and I instantly became friends and his valuable advice flowed continuously, teaching me from the spirit realms. He was so keen to impart as much information as possible to equip me for the work ahead. My mind absorbed everything imparted to me. Any questions I had were instantly answered.

As part of my education, the spirit teachers told me to go and watch other mediums and learn how they handled a service, to learn all the different techniques involved. It was good practice and I learnt a lot. One of the most valuable lessons Tudor taught me was the difference between a medium and a psychic. The medium brings what is known as survival of a life after death. This is normally expected to be personal knowledge known only by the recipient of the messages. A medium or sensitive as we are known mediates with those from the worlds of the spirit, to prove there is such a thing as life after death, that we do and can live on in a spiritual body in a spiritual world, in the same way as we live in a physical world in a physical body. A psychic does not have this ability to mediate between the two worlds. Their job is to work solely on the everyday earthly life of the seeker, helping with such things as problems in daily life and how to resolve them. However, mediums can have all the abilities of mediums and psychics.

There are five different varieties of mediumship - clairvoyance which is seeing the spirit, clairaudience, hearing the spirit, clairsentient, sensing the spirit, trance mediumship, to be in a trance with the spirit power which attempts to overshadow the medium and speak through them, and finally a rare ability known as physical mediumship. This is when the medium, in deep trance, allows the spirits to use all available energy so that those present can see and hear the spirits for themselves. This rare and wonderful ability is opening up completely new areas for those who need more than the spirit worlds normally offer today. I have been privileged to be present at this form of mediumship and found it fascinating.

Tudor passed on countless amounts of information, which I eagerly absorbed and stored for later, when they would be needed. He explained that my work would take a different path later on in my life. In the meantime he showed me the more technical side of our work. He explained it simply and yet although I understood perfectly at the time, I still find it difficult to describe the finer points to others, so I don't bother, I just keep it simple. He also gave me some hints on standing up in front of people.

'Stand up straight, hold your head up high and speak when you have something say. Do not shout when you're in a hall full of people. This is likely only to injure your throat. Tilt your head up and direct your voice to the back of the room. Pace yourself, don't rush your words, they are very important to the congregation.' His voice was never commanding, I could have spent hours listening to him. 'One thing you must do before you begin any spiritual oration is give your audience your biggest smile. You will look approachable, and a pleasant smile will make those about to listen to you feel relaxed. In turn you will feel welcomed. Even more importantly, if you're wrong, tell everyone and then laugh it off. Remember you are human. Hold in your hand something which will give you confidence and prevent you from fiddling. A cross is good or even a bible.' Over thirty-four years later, I still carry something in my hand, and urge others to do the same. Usually it's a stone of some kind. Even if I have had to deal with things in my everyday life, I still hold something which I feel will give me more confidence. 'One other small detail,' he added thoughtfully, 'If you convince one person in the room that night, you have done your work. It doesn't matter if there are 50 or 5000.' Tudor sighed and stepped away from me. That was the end of the lesson for the time being, though he repeated it several times over the months ahead.

I gained such confidence from all he taught me that I worked hard everywhere I went and so many people said such complimentary things about the messages I brought them. Every time I recalled our first meeting in my home, I felt a surge of strength. What pushes me forward are his final words to me, before he moved on to help other new mediums. 'You will help many on this road called life, bringing two together for a brief time.' Knowing I have unusual spiritual gifts and that I can use them to bring loved ones together for a time fills me with total joy.

For some time I felt only the presence of Grey Cloud, an American Indian who has chosen to stay close to me during my lifetime as a medium. He watches over me so that my welfare is always in his hands. His work, at which he is very good, is varied and special, but he does not attempt to work as my guide. His purpose is to encourage my knowledge of spiritual matters, and help people from behind the veil draw close enough to contact their loved ones through me. He is a kind of doorman, though I must add he only organises the spirit side of things. He does not stop anyone from this side coming to talk to anyone in the spirit worlds. However, I wouldn't be able to work at all if spirits kept coming through in any old order. After all, if you visited me hoping your Uncle Fred would come through for a chat and someone else's grandfather came through instead, you wouldn't be very pleased, would you? So Grey Cloud tries to keep order and makes sure he matches up the correct people with the right links on earth. That way I don't have half a dozen spirit people coming through at the same time and confusing the whole process. He's very good at it too. So you see I have adequate protection. Just as well, as not everyone is an angel.

At one point in my education, another American Indian drew closely to me.

'Go to the halls of your learning,' he requested. 'And you will see who I am. For one day you will walk in my footsteps and meet with my family.' I interpreted this as a library. Next time I was in town, I went into the library and I followed the instructions he'd given me. But no matter how I tried, I couldn't find the book he'd suggested. Discouraged, I turned to leave the bay I was searching, tripped over a stool and bumped into the shelves. A book fell out and landed at my feet. Picking it up to replace it in the shelves, I glanced at the title. It was the book I'd been searching for. I opened the pages to be confronted by a photo of a man who was the image of my visitor. He was Wovoka, the leader and last of the Ghost Dancers, who died in 1932, son of Tavibo the prophet, the Messiah of the Paiute tribe.

Shortly after, I was honoured by the presence of what I have since found out was another very great and wonderful Indian. His words to me I will never forget.

'I will fight no more forever.' Tired and weary, he wandered at his leisure around the other helpers. Kindly he stayed for some time before moving on once more, where I do not know. He did seem to have a purpose, though I never discovered it even though we spoke many times before he drifted away. I did not question his moves or reason. It was nothing to do with me. These souls were visitors. Not to stay but, just dropping by to say "Hello".

I read everything I could get my hands on, particularly in relation to symbols and myths. I've learnt over the years that some of the old sayings are idiotic but I still don't like to walk under a ladder or see two knives crossed. Many old sayings have some bearing on mediumship. They crop up occasionally in communication with the spirit people to explain a situation or expression. They are valuable as not all spirits commune in the same way. I found an invaluable book on the subject of the symbolism of flowers and their seasons. So often someone from the spirit realms will offer a single flower and if I know the meaning of it and when it blooms, it often reflects a message, or a month which is important to both the recipient and their loved one in spirit. Tudor explained to me once how some people his side of life have not quite acquired all the ability to talk to a medium and this is a simple way to express themselves until they are able. When they do finally 'find' their voice, you usually can't shut them up.

Despite Grey Cloud's help, I felt lost without Tudor Anderson. The future looked so barren without my old friend. So, when a new source of support came forward, bringing with him the same strength of character as my old tutor, I was cockahoop.

This time, I was introduced to John Redmond, an Englishman. As soon as he first spoke to me, I realised he was no stranger but the owner of the voice which had entered my bedroom in the spray of colour and light when I was seven. The golden tones in his voice wove a blend of love and security round me. John and I would sit for many hours, as I learned from his knowledge. He taught me not to bow before him or any other communicator. I was uneasy about this.

'Surely it shows a lack of respect?' I asked, wondering why such a highly evolved spirit would suggest we could be equals.

'You will show respect to one and all.' His soft brown voice became even warmer as he explained further. 'This builds foundations for the future. We hope such love and respect will build bridges which will link your world to a people who are dedicated to mankind. These bridges will enable far greater contact than the veiled hidden glimpses normally available from your world.' I grew to understand his words and now treat everybody who comes to me from the spirit world in exactly the same way, no matter who they are. It is no hardship as they treat me with exactly the same respect.

'Truth from one soul to another also shows respect,' explained my teacher. 'I represent your soul companion. As your friend we will learn a great deal together before I move back to allow another soul of great warmth and kindness to step in and unveil more spiritual lessons for you and your world to learn by.'

'Move back?' My voice became sad at this news, 'Move back where?'
'Not far,' smiled my mentor.

Into the gap stepped Che Fu Yeng, a Chinese communicator, who encouraged the knowledge locked up in my soul and added his wisdom to mine, wisdom I didn't know I possessed. Gently guided by Che, I walked the path of learning, encouraging in others the blessing of all things spiritual. He stayed with me for many months until he left for other pastures. Quietly he moved away but I knew the band which had brought us together would never be broken, just relaxed.

Soon John Redmond was beside me again, waiting to step back into the breach. His task this time was to encourage confidence. We walked together in this life, within the light of love, with all the blessings of his spirit brethren. We are good friends, and our partnership is as strong now as when he first made his entrance a few years ago.

I was now to learn of a phenomenon known as soul exchange and its amazing results. The spirit guides also endowed me with the ability to allow spirit loved ones to embrace those who go on living in this world. I've seen couples dance together again and hold each other. I've seen feather-light kisses placed on the cheeks of grieving loved ones, with the result that now they grieve no more. My growing education was to teach me that the spirit realms interact with our realms, that they are around us.

I also had help as I started to experiment with different sorts of communication. When I began to understand what 'chakras' are - they are our spiritual centres - Che Fu Yeng returned and helped me understand. He spoke with a direct voice, that is, my voice would disappear and the voice of the spirit would come through. I'll try anything once and, if I don't like it, I'll stop. I chose to stop this, I couldn't see the sense. To some it's of huge value but I didn't like it - it all seemed a bit dangerous.

Beyond these caring souls, I have seen and felt the presence of an even higher brotherhood of souls. They seem to me at certain times, by a nod or shake of the head, to approve or disapprove of some part or other of this way of life. Their gentleness flows like a mighty river of love, so I feel like a child in their presence - learning, making mistakes, doing right, then falling down and hurting my pride, finally standing tall on my own two feet before a band of heavenly masters. I am always trying, pushing through the haze and doing my best for another world beyond the golden horizon. Beyond those that I know of, there is the remainder of the brotherhood. It appears that this is a party of souls that are of an even higher society than I have regularly been aware of. These souls appear in visions of lights. Shining, sparkling like breathtaking flawless diamonds, they are so beautiful. I know I have been in their company. Somewhere deep down inside, I know it, I feel it. I call it soul knowledge. I will face these majestic souls again and I will have passed a test or karma. I hope it will be good news. I couldn't bear to come back, I will not come back and start again, that is, unless it is to help someone who needs a hand in their life.

Chapter Three

How I work

I used to think mediums lived in caravans and wore gypsy clothes. I truly believed they looked up at the ceiling and cried, 'Is there anybody there?' Like everyone, I used to say that in fun. A close friend told me that all Spiritualists and mediums chanted naked around a table, calling up the spirits. She'd seen this done through a split in a curtain in a neighbouring house. I've searched all over this country for a group of naked, chanting spiritualists and, I'm relieved to report, not one of them takes part in anything so risky. They're more likely to ask if you need Spiritual healing or to talk to a medium. Either way they are warming, pleasant and polite, and very respectable. The truth is, mediums are probably the most misunderstood people in the world today. They do NOT have silly cries of 'Is anybody there?' Call, shout, throw a wobbly, whatever they do they cannot summon up spirits on command. When one day I said in fun, 'Is there anybody there?' back came the answer, in equal fun from a group of teenagers in the spirit world, 'No! We're with the WOOLWICH.'

I have demonstrated my work of mediumship in this country and America. Everyone I've met has been most kind and considerate, welcoming me like an old friend. Many spiritualist churches, from tiny rented ones to large ornate buildings, are full of wonderful music. A poem will find its way in, and a visiting medium often reads some inspirational words. Usually I ask if anyone has a 'home-grown' poem they'd like to read to the congregation. An individual will come forward, with either a highly decorated book they have had printed themselves or, in many cases, a lovely poem written on a piece of heavily crumpled paper, dedicated to a loved one and worn down over the years. Never do these priceless works lose their appeal. Spiritualist churches are the only services to my knowledge to include special mention of the animal kingdom and birds, in fact anything, which moves. I like that, it appeals to my sense of perspective.

Because churches book different mediums for their services, each church enjoys a changing stream of attitudes and approaches, benefiting both the unseen worlds and the congregation. The reward to the medium after giving a successful service is a sense of pride in the work and soul satisfaction. I have always striven for this yardstick but also, when befits the moment, I throw in something comical. I find this helps the communication and of course makes sitting down for long periods a little more bearable for a congregation. One thing congregations do very well is laugh at themselves. Then the healing begins.

I am always happy to see people in my home, in churches or meetings, or anywhere else people book me. Any session, wherever it is, first begins in my home where I am helped by the rest of the team from the spirit world. I am surrounded by people who all play a part in the work I do. Although these people are in the spirit world, they have chosen to help me in every way they can. As a team we have a good sense of humour, spending much of our time joking.

The spirit realms aren't all doom and gloom you know. The team gives me all sorts of information which I can use to help all sorts of people, whether they are grieving or are learning like me. My helpers are not around me twenty-four hours a day. Over time I've learnt when to be on duty, and when off. You simply cannot be mentally in the next world around the clock. We still have this life to contend with and its highs and lows. If I spent all my time talking to the invisible worlds, I would be no use to anybody. But when I have work to do, they come into action. I have often felt their presence before an event. Occasionally I have been given information before the telephone rings asking for my help in a particular situation. On many occasions I have been given the names of those about to have startling experiences. It may be weeks before the call comes, but it does come.

Apart from John Redmond and Grey Cloud who are always close at hand, the more day-to-day work is done with spirits like the one I know only as the Secretary. I have never found out whether it's male or female or its name. It organises my time and helps me if I get overtired. I was having a particularly tiring day at my everyday job one day. Work had been very heavy going and I was rushed off my feet. My heart sank when, halfway through the afternoon, I remembered I had two bookings for that evening. I went to the sink and let the water run - water is a force to quick communication. As it ran, I thought 'I just can't do it tonight.' I left it at that and finished off the day's chores. When I got home, the red light on the answer phone was winking at me. Both messages were cancelling that evening's appointments, one woman explaining she'd been given unexpected tickets for the theatre, the other a young man apologising that he couldn't make it that evening. He was a nurse and had been called into work unexpectedly.

The most special of my friends in the spirit realms is a gentle and very spiritual child, who likes to be called Sixpence. Her pastel-colour dresses and matching ribbons contrast with the darkness of her skin. She is so shy but when the corners of her mouth break into a smile, her face beams, while her large dark eyes look through a long fringe. She is so special to me. Her life on earth was horrible, so I think she has adopted me as an aunt. Some time ago I was able to prise some information out of her as to how long she had inhibited the spirit world. Coyly she raised her finger to her mouth then awkwardly giggled as she tried hard to recall. 'Long time' was all she would tell. Only on one occasion did Sixpence reveal to me what had taken her to a world of spirit people.

Tearfully and quietly she spoke of her life in the Deep South of America. She described the older white girl aged about 12 years, whose marriage to a wealthy landowner three times her age brought misery to everyone in his power. Unable to consummate the marriage, the husband found as a companion for his very young wife, a small black girl aged about 7 years - Sixpence. Although Sixpence has suggested to me that her mistress was not strong mentally or physically, she was certainly a very good friend. Sixpence did not need to do the chores which other slaves were born to do, hers was a comfortable life compared to many.

The problem began early in her stay with the master and young mistress, as time after time her master drank something from what Sixpence described as a flask. One night, falling about in a drunken stupor, the master haphazardly made his way to the barn where Sixpence slept. He fell heavily on top of poor Sixpence, who endured the abuse in silence, afraid of what he would do to the other slaves in the barn if she woke them.

For weeks, Sixpence bore the brunt of his excesses, which were fuelled by his inability to enjoy anything approaching a normal married life with his young wife. Sixpence became more and more subdued around the house, only shaking her head in terror when her young mistress asked if she could help. Sixpence knew this was something she must not talk about. Everyone knew their masters used slaves in this way but it was also understood that it must never be mentioned. Fear of the coming night preyed daily on Sixpence's mind. She sent up silent prayers of thanks on the nights when he was too drunk to stagger as far as the barn. She thought of fleeing. She'd heard of slaves finding freedom but she also knew what would happen to her if she were caught. Old One-foot Jason was a daily reminder, and he'd been lucky to survive the flogging.

One blissful period of six days without him staggering in made her realise just how dreadful her life had become. Gradually as the days sped by and she remained free of his attention, Sixpence began to regain something of her old happiness. Whether this served to bring Sixpence once more to his attention, she cannot tell me. All she could eventually bring herself to say was that, that night, he lurched into the barn once more. All the old terror of the pain awaiting her filled Sixpence. She knew she couldn't stand it anymore.

'No,' she cried out. The master stared at her, then raised his hand and sent her flying across the barn to crash into the far wall. Pulling a whip off the horse stand, he strode across to where Sixpence was trying to find her feet. All she could remember was the first lash as it hit her across her shoulders. After that, as she told me the rest of her tale, her eyes filled with tears and she just shook her head when I pressed for details. All she could remember, she insisted, was pain after pain, far worse than anything he'd previously done to her, then silence, darkness and eventually a wonderful light and the beautiful garden where she now lives.

Some people may ask why should a child like that want anything to do with a white person after what had happened to her. It could be because I strongly detest any abuse to any child whether they are black or white. Sixpence sometimes seems to have some one called Mammy with her. I do not know if this is her mother or a person associated with the events of her past. Another thing I have found a little odd is that, whenever another person 'sees' a child with me, this child is always white, with long fair ringlets under a bonnet, a pretty dress which only comes down under her knees and she is very silly, but then she is only about 12 years old. Could this perhaps be Sixpence's young mistress?

Sixpence is an exceptional child of the spirit with the most amazing strength. She works with me to help those spirits who are lost and wander the earth. We have been in many tight corners but she comes up trumps every time, always seeing the situation through to the bitter end.

Over the years, others from the spirit realms have helped me with various aspects of my work, for which I have always been so thankful. Their help has got me out of all kinds of scrapes, whether it's been clearing houses of awkward squatting spooks or helping me understand new areas of my path. One thing which was overlooked when they decided I should take on this role of medium, I AM AFRAID OF THE DARK. I'm always first up the stairs to bed, and don't like being on my own. Worst of all is turning out the light at bedtime and running as fast as I can, in case someone's under the bed and ready to grab my feet, pulling me under with them. Yet I have no problem facing an unsavoury character, spirit or earthling. Stupid, isn't it? Totally illogical, but I just can't help it. And yes, my family think it's silly as well, but that doesn't help.

I also work as a teaching medium for the spirit world. Let me explain. There are mediums who may not have been born yet, but those who will become their spiritual guides are learning to working through existing mediums all the time. The spirit worlds use me for this purpose. These trainee spirit guides try working with me in many different ways which allows them to see first hand what it's like, so that they have some experience before beginning work with their own mediums.

Many people ask why I have such a wide circle of souls around me. I really don't know. It may be because I cover so many areas in this work. It may also be because I am not afraid to try something new. So I can chat to a wide variety of different spirits and learn from them all. I may never see them again but I know they will be somewhere around if I ever need their particular expertise. Some people ask me if I talk to my own relatives. Of course I do, and of course I don't hold them here longer than they need to. I have learned to let go, allowing them the freedom to come and go as they please, knowing they will return later when they are ready.

During the time I am preparing for a sitting, whether it is with one person or in front of hundreds, I am often given the golden opportunity to 'see' in advance whom 'they' need to go to. The spirit world knows who will be coming to see me, indeed often they have directed a relative to come to a meeting. So I'll be given a mind picture of a sister, mother or other relative, who will be coming, hoping for a message from a spirit loved one. You may ask how the spirits know who is going to church on that particular occasion. All loved ones know of your attempts to find solace. You may have thought, 'I feel like going to church tonight, I haven't been for an age'. What was actually happening was that your loved ones were nudging you towards going, because they have a message for you. This may not be evident on your first visit if the spirit cannot connect with the particular medium that night; they may have to wait until another one comes along to communicate that message. Meetings can be so busy that some spirits really find it quite difficult so they wait for a quieter opportunity.

As most students of the paranormal will be aware, some schools of thought suggest that it is imperative that we meditate to enable the spirit realms to draw close enough for basic communication. This is one particular area that I have tried with all my might to do, and I always fail. I have never been able to perform what is considered basic meditation. However, as John Redmond once said to me, it is far better to concentrate than meditate, as your mind and the mind of the spirit beings need to marry up for successful communication.

'If you are meditating, we have to wait for your return,' he added, 'And it is not always a fruitful blessing of minds. Therefore, do try to concentrate.' So I always concentrate deeply to enable another mind to become entwined with mine. I never go into any form of sleep or trance, but chat as the session progresses, explaining what's happening, describing the scene around us and of course, passing on any comments or suggestions from the spirits.

Much of my work takes place in front of crowds of people. It's nerve-racking but very enjoyable and rewarding to work and then be complimented on your high standards in these circumstances.

I have worked several times in the city of Bath, the famous old Roman town, for a church whose chairperson is a lady called Brenda. She retired from the theatre to manage the well-attended modern church, making it one of her chief priorities in life. She has turned it into one of the country's most respected and well-used venues where the very best mediums and healers have worked.

Brenda, an expert on the history of mediums, told me that I worked like the mediums at the turn of the century, first bringing loved ones through, then the spirit guides, for those people in the congregation. Because this was so rare, she publicly told the waiting congregation that they had heard the English mediums and now they would hear the cream of all Britain, a Welsh medium.

At first I felt humbled, then quite embarrassed. But Brenda wouldn't give up.

'You have what is known as charisma,' she explained. 'That is a gift in itself.' I felt so awkward but this feeling soon went as I began to work, pouring out messages one after another to the waiting crowd. When I had finished, a great surge of people came forward trying to speak to me. 'Thank you,' and 'When are you coming again?' I heard all around me. Brenda came to my rescue, telling everyone to wait and that I may speak to one or two later after a cup of tea upstairs in the tearooms. Suddenly there were just a few of us left in the church, so, thinking everyone else had gone home, I made my way upstairs for a nice cuppa.

Opening the door to the upstairs room, I was besieged by waiting people who made a rush toward me. It was more frightening than taking a service. Along came Brenda again and handled the scene brilliantly. I got my tea, they got their questions answered. All's well with the world and God's in his heaven.

You may think that this kind of image could easily make me bigheaded, but I have always felt humbled by those who praise my work and me. If I am praised, those who work with me as a team in the spirit body are praised also. And so they should be. They work so hard to make people happy, both sides of the veil. I am a go between and that's all.

I also work through postal readings. People send me photos of themselves surrounded by loved ones who are now in the spirit world. I then write back with messages which are filtered from your loved ones through my guides. Sometimes it works the other way. A spirit will turn up with a photo and a message for a loved one still on earth, particularly if they know their relative does not attend any church or know a medium to work through. But I would never get in touch with anybody down here if I were given a message for them from the spirit world. If the spirits want to get through to their loved ones here, I insist they get their relatives who are still earthside to come to me. It is not for me to intrude unasked on anybody's grief.

I can also have contact through psychometry which is the art of reading through an instrument. I found this art quite by accident. It seems that any inanimate item can be read just like reading a book. The person using this method can find out where the item originated from and even tell who handled the particular object. Running anything through your fingers prompts images to form in the mind's eye. Describe what you see and it's possible that with practice anyone can become quite proficient in the art of psychometry.

My first run-in with this strange form of reading came when I was playing a game of darts with my husband at a local public house. After a few games, another couple joined us. We didn't know one another but soon got chatting and it was then that things began to get a little odd. Each time I had to take the darts out, I seemed to see scenes not belonging to Keith's life or mine.

I seemed to be able to see into a bank, then I named it. I could see the chap I was playing darts with. I could tell that while he had worked in the bank that afternoon, he'd been having problems with a long series of numbers which were written down on paper. I could easily see the mistake he'd been making and told him so. He was fascinated by what I said, and asked me how I knew he worked in a bank as we had only just met. He also wanted to know how I knew he had a problem? I shrugged my shoulders and suggested he let me know if my insight had benefited him at all. I didn't have to wait long.

'You were correct,' he admitted, when I bumped into him a few days later. 'I did have a problem adding the figures up.' He begged me to tell him how I had known the bank's business so well, as he had not mentioned his worry to anyone.

'Don't play darts with a medium,' I laughed and walked on leaving him open-mouthed.

Perhaps the most interesting occasion when I used psychometry related to an incident which happened over eighty years ago.

A young couple drove long and hard from England to see me. They knew I couldn't promise to help them but I told them before they cam that I would certainly try.

Bob and Sheila were only in their twenties, and as their story unfolded I became as keen as they to find answers to their questions. They were a brother and sister who'd been researching their family tree. They were hoping I could help them with one particular hiccup they had come across. Sheila produced a small package which immediately gained my full attention. However once I saw what was inside the package, I became convinced it was a send up. All that was revealed was a button. They quickly assured me they were very serious indeed. Once I was convinced, I asked Sheila not to touch the button more than she had to, as that would obscure the view I hoped to get of its owner.

'It belonged to our uncle,' explained Sheila. 'When he died, it was taken off his coat by his friend who was also an undertaker.'

I held out my hand to receive the button. The minute Sheila put it into my hand, scenes ran through my mind like a TV screen showing a film. I saw a short man who held government office in another country. I had never seen this country before in my life, yet somehow I knew it was Ireland. A clear scene showed a statue or water fountain in the centre of a rough road surrounded by bushy low-growing trees. Suddenly a noise and the flash of a gun. The man lay dead. His attacker had hidden behind the greenery and was gone long before I was able to identify him.

I homed in on the dead man's face, still twisted in pain as blood soaked out from his chest and through his coat. A button caught the sunlight. Suddenly I was staring at the button inside the undertaker's office. Bob and Sheila confirmed that their uncle had been murdered over eighty years earlier. But they were desperate to know where he had died. I knew the answer was County Cork Ireland.

Some months later they phoned to say that, thanks to my abilities, they had managed to get their uncle's death certificate. He had indeed been killed in County Cork Ireland at the turn of the last century.

This odd gift has brought sadness and laughter, no more so than with one lady who brought something personal for me to hold. In this case however, her late mother chose to join in the conversation. I explained to my client that her mum was close by and would like to talk to her but as often happens, the daughter found it difficult to accept that her mother really was at the side of us and shrugged it off as impossible.

'Well, my dear,' said the mother, 'Those pearl earrings and necklace you sneaked in through Customs were not a figment of my imagination, were they?' Her daughter's face was a picture. 'No-one knew about that, not even my husband,' she blabbered, grabbing her things and making a dash for the door. 'I'll have to go, I've left something on the stove.' In her hurry, she bumped straight into the door and dropped everything. Scrabbling round on the floor to pick them up, she paused only long enough to stare balefully at me. 'You are peculiar' then banged the door shut behind her.

On a lighter note this gift can be useful if I am called when a family pet goes missing. You may laugh at this area of mediumship but many families and individuals go through sleepless nights because the dog has decided to go walkabout.

Heather phoned me in the hope that her dog could be found, safe and well.

'Bring something belonging to your dog and I will see if I can get anything on him,' I advised. I treat each case exactly the same whether it involves a human or an animal. Heather turned up for her appointment laden with two bags of blankets, combs, brushes, collar and leads, not forgetting a huge assortment of toys.

I picked up the brush, and stared out of my window into my garden. Suddenly I heard a voice from the spirit realms. It was Heather's father who had departed many years ago. The elderly gentleman showed me pictures in my mind's eye of a housing estate on the other side of town. Large gates surrounded a private building on the edge of the estate, near a skip laden with building material. I was able to home into a bundle of what looked like rags. Suddenly it started shaking, then I could hear pining. It was Heather's dog.

'Go to this area and your dog will be there,' I smiled. The relief in her face and voice said it all.

'Thank you so much,' she sobbed, choking back the tears. 'You must think I'm silly crying over my dog like this but I can't help it. And it's just so wonderful that Dad came through for me. He knows how much that mutt means to me.' Her tears dried up, she set off to fetch her dog which she found exactly where I'd said he'd be, tired and starving but alive and safe.

Having the finest team in the spirit realms certainly helps me. Their patience is unlimited. Furthermore, they have a knack of bringing me down to earth when I go above my station in this work.

My confidence had reached an all-time high, and taking a service was a doddle. However, I forgot the golden rule, respect for my peers in spirit, and also humility, which is the next commandment. A young boy in spirit informed me that I was about to have the rug pulled from under me. The spirit realms had to teach me that as a medium I needed them for the process of communication just as they needed me, for the same process. We work as a team, they bring the correct spirit for the correct relative or friend, offering messages to the correct person on earth from the correct spirit. I did not heed the warning, and gave the wrong information to the wrong person. What a fool I made of myself that day, thinking I could do this work without the full co-operation of the guides, just the thing to bring any medium down to earth with a bump! If at any time I or any other medium feel that we are confident enough to work without the aid of the spirit realms at the wheel, everything can go wild. Now I always begin with the guides, never on my own.

Of course I make mistakes. The human element rides side-saddle with the spiritual, and I readily admit this when I go wrong. My usual comment is, 'Oh, oh, guess what I've done. Scrub that!' This always brings howls of laughter from my audience, because I am usually falling about laughing with them also. You have to laugh - I do it all the time. It gets boring otherwise. I often wonder if maybe it's my sense of humour that attracts the spirits to me. My gifts are something to take joy in and pleasure is such an important part of life. I always know when I have given my all in a reading or service. I am starving. I could eat anything in sight. No wonder I'm so round, it's the spirit world using up my spiritual energy.

I never write anything down about any session, wherever it takes place. The temptation to look up what I have already told somebody, if they visit me again, could be too great, which isn't fair on the people who are coming to see me again, perhaps in the hope of hearing something new. I always take each session afresh and I can't recall ever failing, which is of course a pressure in itself. My lack of notes has also meant this book has perhaps been harder to write than it would have been if I'd kept a diary. My memory for places and dates is hazy. But at least it means that what I have remembered to put into this book are the more outstanding episodes of my incredible life.

So many have benefited from what the spirit realms have programmed for me. Not once have they let me down, always vibrant in their work, truthful and reliable. What better friends could anyone ask for? Quietly they move around in the background, always supporting me and on hand for anything dealt out. 'They' really make me feel so humble. If only people could understand the work and dedication put in by so many people, they would, I'm sure, feel as I do. Content!

I enjoy my work, and feel so grateful when the special one you hope to come through does so, right on target with their information. It's so simple. By offering information about a loved one in spirit and giving messages from them, I hope that the grieving process can be halved or even relieved, so that we can get on with our lives. Not to forget, far from it, just to know that they are only a smile away, or even a tear.

I once heard of an old gentleman who had lost his beloved wife after many years together. The wife had died unexpectedly on the operating table. Soon afterwards, the late wife appeared to her husband. When I was told of this, I rushed to offer my condolences, only to be met with the old man's son, a vicar, who had told his father that his late mother could not possibly have reappeared. I didn't think it appropriate to say what I would normally have said so I just told them that they should remember her as if she had not gone anywhere and was only a memory away.

What a shame these old fallacies exist. Think how these people could get on with their lives, instead of becoming ill with grief. With this knowledge, son and father could have got on with their lives. Instead, the old man passed over to the spirit world shortly after and the man of the cloth plodded on, blind-folded as before.

I have never intended to cause anyone extra grief. I feel it's enough that they manage to handle what is dealt out to them. Instead, I do believe that people like me have a path to walk in this life, and that we soften the blow of death if people are open-minded enough to know that there is no death, just a doorway which we all go through. No one is immune, no matter what their colour or creed. Some people are helped by Christian beliefs, other by different faiths. But the spirit realms showed me where the truth lies. If our god is high on a mountain peak, we all need to take a road to get to him. Some will take a different path from us. Others will think they have the only correct route, but we will all find God at the top in the end. Some reach him sooner than others but we all find our way at the closing of our day.

I have found over the years that walking under a canopy of old trees brings a basic force which fills me with a strength, a super build up of love energy to work for the spirit realms. Just strolling within the green pastures of the countryside fills me with such clean vigour that I am often able to carry out large amounts of spiritual work. I never fail to first ask the great giant of a tree if I may take some of its energy, and always thank my benefactor after. Filled with a clean almost magical healing, I am able to cope with whatever comes next.

After that first session in the Spiritualist Church, quietly my name got around. I was booked in at some of the loveliest churches. Often they were only rented rooms - I like to call them churches in suitcases, as they only meet once or twice a week - set up for the purpose of holding a service but they are no less beautiful than any other venue. There was one church which looked like Dr. Who's Tardis. From the outside, it looked as if it would be full if three people stood with their arms around one another. No room for the spirit realms in this one, I thought. But when I entered what I thought was a garden shed, the sight which met my eyes was stunning. Lavender-blue-covered chairs and blush-pink walls first, then a podium set further up the aisle. Its brass rails mirrored the lights and reflected the colours surrounding it. It was dazzling. On the subject of auras I have always found it pleasing to the eye when I enter a church of spirits. The colours range from pinks to penetrating blues and back to lavender hues, each one vibrating around and within the building, beating like a heartbeat as other splendid colours display their warmth over the building. How spiritual these venues are, how peaceful their sounds against the hurdy gurdy of life outside their framework. All who enter the doors become aware of this healing, if not in the singing then in the tranquil setting, waiting for the spirit people to arrive.

Standing up in front of a crowd and speaking off the cuff is no mean feat. Let's remember I have no script to learn, no one to urge me on from the earth if I go mentally blank. However I have one advantage over many who speak in public. I had the company of angelic souls whose main purpose is to offer messages through me, messages which encourage laughter in place of tears.

Of course I can understand when someone is frightened of what I have said. It can be unbelievable when someone you know has died and then a person like me comes along and shakes you to your foundations by repeating what that spirit person has said to me.

And that is what happened many years ago when three women made an appointment to see me. The oldest one of the three was quite satisfied when her late brother came through with convincing information and words of comfort. He had drowned in a nearby river. Through his eyes I was able to see his lifeless body floating downward through the water.

One of the others, a young lady, shook with a mixture of disbelief and happiness. Her little daughter had died at birth, the cord had strangled her. But there was a spirit lady called Sarah also present whom I was interested in. She fluttered around the child, never moving too far away from her side. When I mentioned Sarah's name, gasps of disbelief broke the air.

'That was my mother in law,' sobbed the young mum.

'Well,' I smiled, 'Your little girl is being looked after by her grandmother and very well too.' The look of joy on the mother's face was wonderful to see.

It was now the turn of the last young woman. A man aged about twenty years stepped forward into my sight. He was a bit sheepish in talking but quickly gave his name and some personal information.

'It's Billy,' he said as I passed on the rest of the information.

'No, no,' she cried out, turning to me. 'Someone must have told you his name.

How else could you have known this information? You're a fraud.' Her friends had told the poor mite that she was going to have her fortune told. What a shock for her, to find all these people coming through, even her childhood friend, Billy, whose death had been so sudden. She was so shocked that she got up from the chair and ran to the other side of the room, well away from me.

'Who told you? You couldn't have known, you couldn't have.'

'I'm sorry if it's a shock but there's no way I could have got that information except from Billy himself. I have abilities....' But her hands were over her ears and she refused to listen any more.

Responsible mediums only want to pass on correct information which can sometimes be hard to get from a spirit. But when correct information is delivered to the recipient and people misunderstand, it is terrible.

I was booked to work in a church in the valleys of Wales. Messages came thick and fast, spirit loved ones lining up to talk for a little while with their loved ones. One father came through, giving me masses of information about himself and his family to pass on to his daughter. But she didn't seem to understand.

'I know what will do the trick,' he told me. 'Tell her I was there when she bought her new car.' He gave me the make and the number. As I passed it on to his daughter, her eyes grew round and she screamed.

'Oh my God, I'm going to have an accident. I knew I should never have bought a green car.' Vainly I tried to explain.

'No-one's said anything about an accident, love. These details are only some sort of evidence, just to prove to you that your father was there when you bought the car. He just wants you to know that he is always close to you even though he is out of sight.' Only then did she seem to accept that I was only doing what every medium tries to do - deliver greetings from a loved one.

About this time, I started seeing a blue flashing light. One day, I was taking a sitting in a house in Cardiff when I 'saw' Jack Warner of 'Dixon of Dock Green' fame.

'I'll be dropping in over the next few months,' he told me, 'I'm very interested in your type of work.'

Maureen whose house it was, was ecstatic but I needed proof, I don't take things at face value. However, that proof wasn't long in coming. Maureen and I had joined a group which went to London for talks, the next one of which quickly came round. This one was on the subject of 'Famous old mediums'. The speaker slotted a slide in to illustrate his next point and there was Jack Warner, staring out of the screen. I know my mouth dropped open and I guess so did Maureen's. She nudged me.

'Is that who I think it is?'

'Yes it is,' I whispered back.

The man giving the lecture glared in our direction so we subsided. But I couldn't take my eyes off the screen.

'My wife and I were on holiday,' droned on the speaker, 'When we bumped into Jack Warner and his wife. We spent a great afternoon chatting. Jack Warner said his wife Molly was a medium and she had a little spirit lad as a guide.' I was so stunned I didn't take in any more of his talk. Once we got outside afterwards, Maureen and I just burst out together.

'Wasn't that amazing?' and 'What a wonderful experience.'

Jack Warner did visit me a couple of times after that and was always very friendly, very caring and compassionate. I learned he had never taken a script in this world unless Molly's spirit guide had said to accept it.

'You'll always know when I'm going to appear,' he told me. 'You'll see my blue light.' After a few months, he stopped visiting. He'd presumably gone off to learn about another area of our work.

It's not always in order to communicate with relatives and friends in the spirit world that people come to see me. Sometimes they need guidance in their path in this world. The young lady was only in her twenties and her long auburn hair shone like an aura around her small round face. I had no idea why she had come to see me so I asked the spirit guides for some help.

'Does she have boyfriend problems?' I asked. John Redmond shook his head. 'Does she need to know her job prospects?' Again he shook his head, smiling in a way that was beginning to annoy me. 'Tell me what the child needs,' I almost commanded him. To my amazement I could see a nun, her red hair hidden under a head-dress of dark cloth, her small build drowned under a dress of black cloth.

I looked at the girl who was keeping her eyes averted from mine. She just stared at the floor but I could tell she was listening avidly as I told her that, although I had been called to the life I lead, life has other pathways too. For some, that pathway is to carry the banner of God. She raised her pale blue eyes and searched my face in surprise.

'How did you know that's all I want to do? I've tried so hard to resist the call. I've even tried being like my friends and going out with them to pubs and clubs but it's never any good. I always feel so empty when I return to my flat that I spend the rest of the night crying and praying for guidance. But I still don't know what to do.'

'Have you tried talking to anyone about this?' She shook her head. She had no idea who could advise her as to her correct spiritual path. In fact it is difficult, if not impossible, for anyone other than the spirit worlds to advise people on these matters.

'Well, John?' I asked, 'What do you advise in this situation, my wise friend?' John's answer was so simple.

'Her life is preordained, she has a mission. There are many people waiting for her good and gentle works. She was not born for mate and child but a spiritual life spent caring for others in other lands. Tell her to follow her soul's voice and she will find a great deal of happiness, more than most ever could.' I passed on exactly what John had told me. Her relief at hearing these words was so great that I felt pretty good too. It is not up to mediums to make decisions for others; it may change a life forever. I leave these matters up to those in the know, my spirit guides.

The examples I will go into are as memorable to me now, as they were when they first became part of my life. I have, when necessary, changed the names of those who have become a part of this book. The incidents remain as accurate as possible. Some are documented in other books, but remain true and confidential, unless permission by those involved has been given. I am always, when relating these stories, very aware of clients' feelings.

Chapter Four
Summerlands

The first question everyone asks is what's the spirit world like? If I were to devote a whole book to describing the worlds of the spirits, I couldn't do it justice. After all, how could we cover all the towns and cities of this world in one chapter, or even in one book? That's the scale of the task if I had to describe the Summerlands and that I certainly could not do. But there are some pointers I can give you.

The spirit world is similar to Earth but more colourful and less demanding. There are many layers, through which spirits progress upwards or downwards as they mature. If we understand that the earth is a training school, we can easily understand that we are all at varying levels of that education. Some are in kindergarten, coming to terms with anything spiritual. Others, in higher schools of thought, have their lives enriched by deeper understanding of all things spiritual. Of course there are those who know that this life is but a few moments in time and that we have a need to return home to our soul's birth land with everything we have learned and experienced intact.

When we return to the spirit home, we all arrive at the same level. It is afterwards that we forge ahead into other realms more suited to our needs. Then we understand the full meaning of life and why we had the lessons we did. Some may have known only the lesson of pain - this can only be felt on earth. We cannot feel this emotion of suffering while in a spirit body, only the earth holds this function.

I have seen only a small portion of the spirit worlds and could not begin to guess at the rest. Whenever I have visited the spirit realms, I have been aware of green rolling meadows. It is always warm where I have been invited, though there is another area worth a mention. There is a land which only knows snow, but the snow does not turn to slush. Intermittent snowflakes gently caress your cheek as they fall quietly to the ground. You don't need extra clothing as the snow is not so cold that it burns your hands or blinds your eyes. But it is still snow. There are also areas which know only autumn, though its colours are not to be found on Earth.

The higher the sphere the more intricate the design of its structures. Crystal and glass-like cities sparkle with the spirit sun, producing rainbow colours which dance round and about the prism-like tower buildings. But the air is keen here for those who try to enter this realm before they are far enough advanced spiritually. This encourages them to return to realms which are better suited to their current progress.

I have seen a portion of the lower realms and they contain no fire. Instead, a thick choking air exists there. If you can imagine the horror of putting your face into a bag of maggots, you're somewhere close to the feeling of the air which scraps along the rocks and dark passageways of these low levels. There's a strong feeling of being watched, a sense of a presence, then a suffocating overwhelming feeling that you're trapped. It is so cold and dark that whichever way you turn you are lost. Mix all that with total fear and terror. Have you smelt fear? It is not nice. I was told that this place was quite pleasant compared to other levels. Needless to say, I did not venture lower than this level – it was quite enough for me. Of course it is impossible for inmates to escape as they would not be able to breathe the cleaner air of higher levels, including the air of Earth.

The inhabitants of these lower levels can always improve their mental and spiritual state but few make this effort, preferring to dwell in a world bereft of emotion. Their souls contain neither kindness nor compassion. It's hard work for them even to decide to improve. But there is help available to them. Some spirits choose to work as rescuers in these realms to improve the progression of their own souls. This Samaritan effort is the ultimate test for good spirits. This area is too large to open up in this chapter, and unless anyone is planning to venture into these realms I suggest we leave it alone.

So what happens when a soul passes over into the Summerlands? Most manage to walk freely into the spectacular welcoming lights displayed by loving attentive souls whose only desire is to welcome a tired traveller weary from the fight of this life. They are then put into familiar caring homes or hospitals.

All they have to do is enjoy the soothing lights which encourage sleep, while the air and the colours perform the necessary spiritual healing. The soul is refreshed and often surprised to find that it still breathes. And why not? We do it all our lives; it's a little difficult to stop. But souls breathe in a beautiful air of love and care and peace. The love is contagious and you cannot help but return the same affection to all around you.

People in the Summerland are far more friendly, caring, interested in you, the person. However, if you enjoy your own company and feel that you need some time to settle in, of course this is accepted. You do not feel a prisoner; you're free to roam whenever and wherever you wish. There are no limitations to what you are able to do and only those who loved us on Earth are our visitors. Everyone who loved us on the earth, family or friends, we meet again in the spirit world. As long as happiness was the main ingredient in the relationship, we see everyone again, including animals.

Once you are ready to explore your newfound surroundings, there will always be someone who you may feel is familiar and comforting, even though you may not recall seeing them on the earth. This is probably because, before you decided to go to the earth, you were the best of friends, and they volunteered to guide you, hoping you would at some stage recall a friend who cared for you, just out of sight.

Shortly after a soul returns to the spirit realms, there is a time when they return to earth for a while. Then they seem to go away for a period of time to explore the worlds around them. This period introduces them to lives they had before this one and gives them a chance to meet again those who were part of their lives, like school friends and old pals long gone on. It's a time to walk through places which bring good memories, to sit with those who have the gift of music or art, to be taught the ways of the spirit realms, to visit loved ones on earth all over again, to inspire them to move on in their lives and to show them that we will and can all be together again one day. There is no second death to separate those we love and who have loved us.

People often ask me how those in the higher life look. Do they appear ill or sickly? Do they look as if they have been languishing in a state of pure hell? Of course not. Spirit people look just like you and me. Everyone is happy. I have never seen anyone from the spirit worlds look sad or despondent. They appear so content as if they now know all the answers and are very pleased and relieved.

The soul is perfect, no defects mar the appearance. In fact I have seen within hours those who have passed away, leaving a worn out body. When they have made their return, they look better than some people I have seen still on earth. Health problems which affected you on earth will disappear in the spirit worlds. If for instance you suffered a chest condition all your life, which stopped you going out into the pollen-laden air, it will never affect you in the Summerlands. Roam wherever you feel, pick flowers, lie down in the grass, and listen to the music of the flowers. All deformities fade with the physical body. The spirit body is perfect. Mental illness is recognised as a problem belonging to the physical brain and makeup. No one condemns them. Instead, they are given an incredible amount of answers. No one is punished if they have chosen to end their own life on this earth.

Odd things can happen at the time of passing. I once heard of a gentleman who made the wedding cake for his daughter's wedding. Shortly after the wedding the man died. When the cake was cut up, it was found to be a dark green colour. What could have caused this? A young woman called in on her elderly mother, saw her mum take her last breath, and pass over. Quite unexpectedly, the room turned green. What caused this? Effervescence from the departing bodies can leave deposits in surrounding areas, or items tinted with green, although it is not normally so noticeable. Soul shock amongst other things can spark this kind of distress. What is that cold shiver which runs along my arm or neck? Known as love energy, it's a spirit loved one putting an arm around you in comfort. Just say thank you, or hello, mentally. That is all that is needed. I chose to call the energy we feel when a loved one is near, Love Energy. It has all the hallmarks of care and consideration for you. The warmth sent out to you from a loved one or your guide will make you tingle. So next time this happens, tell everyone you're having Love Energy. By the way there is nothing sexual about this experience, just in case anyone asks.

Yes, there is work to do in the world of the spirit, but only if you feel you could work. It is not heavy demanding work as we have on earth but joyful work, which brings happiness to those we inhabit the worlds with. You have more time to enjoy your surroundings, to absorb the healing colours which permeate the air. More than likely you will recognise where you are when you go to the spirit realms. You will find familiar streets and houses accommodating familiar people.

There is a stage which more highly progressed spirits reach where they are less genderised than any of us could imagine. They are not man or woman, but the purest of souls. These, I have been informed, are less likely to be near the earth, so angelic are they that they reach instead toward the godhead and an infusion of love you or I would not be able to envisage. Instead we would be likely to be reduced to tears at the sheer beauty and gentleness of their presence. They are truly holy, abiding in a realm so sacred that only the pure of heart have ever been close to this paradise.

One thing is certain. We need to love one another as human beings. All who enter the higher realms feel only love for one another. That is the one thing which helps us on our road to a more progressive society, a higher plane of existence. How can we be part of the ultimate intelligence we call God if we do not know how to love one another? It is not difficult to show kindness to one another. It is then that we strive to be better people and can take our place among those who will love us.

The words 'spirit guides' and 'Spirit Companions" are the same, and neither has wings nor floats about on fluffy white clouds. Nevertheless, they are special in every sense of the word, caring souls who hold back on their own progression so they can help you and me. Why should some one we have never met do this for us? Are they waiting to be paid, you might ask yourself? No. These souls who watch and try hard to guide us are chosen for their love of us. Sometimes our loved ones are our guides. If we have a special mission in this life, we attract the spirit to us who would be best suited for this work. Highly evolved souls who may have been in a profession themselves will feel the need to help. The medical profession is typical of guiding souls who inspire and encourage strength in those who need the most help at their disposal. Musicians are always looking for inspiration, and often a spirit will fill the void. I must explain that we are not puppets; freewill is and always has been the way forward.

I always thought that when I returned to the spirit realms, my life as a medium would end. After all 'they' will all be over there with me at that time. So what would I do to fill the void? Why, I would be expected to assist in helping the guides with a new medium on the earth. I am looking forward to that.

I need every now and again to ask the most unusual questions of the spirit realms such as, what do funeral directors do when they return to the spirit world!! Back came the answer, whatever they feel they did not have the time for when involved in their 'work'. Some may enjoy golf. For others, it may be drama classes, to another, meeting those who they looked after before the long journey. Another question burning a hole in my thoughts was, do spiders survive the transition to the spirit world? Back came the answer, everything and everyone survives. Including spiders. Ugh! And just one other thing, could I still enjoy a bag of hot freshly cooked chips? Back came the answer, indeed you can. Hooray. Oh, just one more question, I begged, will I gain more weight in doing so. NO! WOW! I'm ready.

Chapter Five

Homespun spirits

You may think that nothing the spirit world can do would frighten me now. After all, I've had years of experience of visiting spirits, so I should be used to their appearances, shouldn't I? Don't you believe it. I have never professed to being brave. I jump out of my skin at anything unexpected and shudder at cold breezes on otherwise calm balmy days. Even in my own home, things "Happen" which still scare me rigid. Obviously I am mentally and spiritually prepared when I am expecting to see, hear, or feel an apparition but I can't be aware of the other world twenty four hours a day. That just isn't healthy and would be very boring for everyone, especially me, when the rest of the family are enjoying normal everyday events. There's plenty of time to talk to the spirits without them crossing the line to chat with me every five minutes. However, there are of course the exceptions to the rule and occasions when the spirits need to speak to me for some reason, I'm ready.

On this particular occasion, I had only risen from my warm bed moments before. I'd been awake chatting to Keith and considering showering or dressing but had decided to go and make a cup of tea first. Dressing gown in hand and still talking lightly to Keith, I walked the few steps to the closed bedroom door and opened it halfway. Suddenly I saw a little girl coming out of the morning darkness on the landing. She was no more than eight years old. In her small outstretched hand, she held a simple candlestick. I could only see half the candle but its flame danced in a draught, despite her careful hand shielding it. Her bare feet struggled to kick aside her long white nightdress as she walked slowly along the landing towards me. Her hair was styled in the pudding basin cut of the hungry Thirties. Her gaze left the candle flame and she looked up to the door of the room next to where I was standing. She smiled at whoever welcomed her, then vanished into a tear in the fabric of time, gone from my astonished sight.

My legs refused to move. I forced myself to relax and retreated into the bedroom, closing the door behind me. Then I dashed to the security of bed and husband and dived under the bedclothes, my dressing gown tightly gripped in my hands. My husband, still half-asleep, noticed nothing.

'What's the matter? Thought you wanted a cup of tea?' Only I knew how much I needed that cuppa. He threw back the bedclothes and pulled on a pair of jeans. 'S'pose you expect me to get one for you, do you?' Muttering under his breath, and oblivious to my panic, he made his way over to the door. Holding the door handle, he glanced out to where the ghostly child in white had stood. I held my breath, sure she would have returned, but the landing was empty. She had melted into time. Keith stepped out of view and went downstairs. I fell back onto the bed, relieved that the spirit world had stopped giving me any more shocks. Then my eyes widened as I realised that I was totally alone. I dashed from the bed, made a quick check at the door, and then raced downstairs, much to my husband's amusement. He wasn't used to me being so energetic at such an early hour. I was still shaken but couldn't say anything to Keith. He didn't mind me doing this work as long as I kept it 'contained'. He would not be pleased to find a ghostly figure strolling through our bedroom, even if it was a child. This event occurred some time ago and yet I still walk anxiously up to my bedroom. What was so unnerving was that I had no mental preparation; the whole episode was completely out of the blue.

I always kept my fingers crossed that it would never happen again but of course it did, years later when I was away in the Cornwall. Admittedly, it was only an arm sailing through the air and past my husband's nose. Nothing too horrific! When I returned, he told me to take all the spirits with me next time, not just bits of them.

Many people who live in old houses hear stairs creak or floorboards groan even when no one is walking about the home. One of our problems is not so easily explained. The door separating the kitchen from the living room appears to have a life all of its own. It rattles and vibrates without any breezes and with no one walking about. The knockings are only a problem to us when they bang louder than the television. Sometimes we can't hear ourselves talk. Then we resort to shouting at it to stop, and it immediately does so. But sure enough, we'll hear a final very quiet knock, almost in a cheeky childish way, before complete hush descends. Such spirit antics usually make us dissolve into laughter, which makes the spirit start all over again. Of course others have heard the knockings. They don't seem to stay long, not even for a cup of tea. I often wonder why - with a giggle, of course. I did wonder if the child spirit wants to be a poltergeist when it grows up!

During the time I spent in the USA the door never moved. Not one rattle, knock or movement on the handle. So whoever is playing with the door obviously came with me to the States. I could easily have rescued this spirit and sent it on its way back to where it could be happy, but it seems quite happy and content playing with the door.

Late one evening, I was alone in bed reading, Keith was still downstairs watching television. The bedroom was exceptionally quiet, the street outside seemed to have settled down earlier than usual and I couldn't even hear the TV downstairs. The perfect time and place to say goodnight to the spirit world, to avoid any interruptions from them during the night. I snuggled under the duvet and picked up my book from the bedside table.

Suddenly a voice echoed round the room.
'You have done a lot of good work for us recently, Frances. Enjoy your reward.' My book hit the floor. The space around my bed became filled with people. They had to be spirits - after all, not many people could have Elvis, Indian chiefs and mandarins in their bedroom at the same time! Elvis clearly didn't want to be there - he moved impatiently from one foot to the other, then I heard him say, 'Is this it? Can I get back now please? I've done what I had to do and I'm going.' He disappeared from the throng, but then I recognised another face, this time from television. Yootha Joyce, of 'George and Mildred' fame, was standing with a drink in one hand.

'That looks good,' I joked. 'I didn't realise you could still get alcohol over there.'
'Oh yes,' she drawled in that famous voice. 'I enjoyed it down there so why not up here? Trouble is, the effect's not the same.' So many spirit people visited me that evening. It was a truly wonderful experience and a reward I certainly enjoyed.

The spirit realms can still leave me wide-eyed at the incredible power which occasionally they display not just for me but for anyone in my company at the time. One night after Keith and I had a disagreement, I stormed up to bed. Not to the marital bed, but to the bed of our youngest daughter Samantha, who was 14 at the time. Her bedroom was in darkness, except for a dim light which just reached the window from a street lamp a few yards away from the house. Closing the bedroom door quietly behind me, I tried not to wake her as I crept over to the bed. Despite my care, she woke up.

'What's the matter, Mum? Is there something wrong? Why aren't you in your own bed?'

'Don't worry, love,' I answered quickly, 'I'm just not speaking to your father at the moment. Let's just go to sleep.' Reassured, Sam settled back under the duvet and I curled up alongside her. As my eyes began to close, a grey mist seemed to appear and I shook my head to clear my sight. But the mist spread further into the room from the door. Beginning to panic in case it was smoke and the house was on fire, I sat upright in bed and pulled Sam tight.

'Don't worry,' I reassured her as I realised there was no smell of smoke. Whatever it was, at least the house wasn't on fire. Though I tried to remain outwardly relaxed for Sam's sake, I was petrified and the panic was overwhelming.

'What is that, Mum? Where did it come from?'
'Hush,' I whispered as my stomach turned somersaults and the pounding in my chest grew louder. The mist became denser. What was obviously a vortex of energy moved slowly, weaving itself inside out, yet not moving from around the door. 'Quick', I urged Sam, 'Look out of the window. Maybe something's reflecting from the street lamp into the room.' Sam crawled out of bed on the side away from the mist and scuttled across to the window.

'There's nothing out there which could possibly be that,' she whispered as she raced back to the bed and jumped under the covers. 'Anyway the street lamp's gone out and all the houses opposite are in darkness.' My stomach lurched in terror. I clutched Sam's hand and we clung together, just so glad I wasn't alone.
The darkness in the room became intense, the only light coming from the swirling band of greyish fog. Gradually the mist peeled away to reveal a cross which stood upright, filling the width and breath of the door. A great light, hazy but brilliant, yet not hurting our eyes, expanded upwards from the bottom of the cross. Up and up it grew, brighter and brighter, throwing off its coat of grey

cloud. We were mesmerised, looking at the biggest widest cross we had ever seen. It had no support, yet touched the full height of the door and spanning some five feet across. The light grew brighter, becoming even more intense but not blinding our eyes. Fascinated, we watched as shadows of people, dwarfed by the mighty cross, walked around its base.

I was aware of the purest feeling of peace cascading around us, uniting us, followed by a wave of love which made us feel so safe. All we wanted to do was return that love.

The vision stayed for some moments before slowly fading behind a veil separating the two worlds. In its place remained an atmosphere so tranquil that we didn't speak for a while, then we fell into a sound sleep.

If that isn't the most spiritual display ever offered by those in the spirit world, I don't know what is. Today some twenty years later Sam and I still talk of the White Cross of light. Everything about this cross represented something sacred and holy, telling us that we, Sam and I, were protected and loved by a mighty force which was both larger and stronger than anything I have ever known.

My own religious beliefs are quite basic. For many years I fought with this question, my views changing like the weather, before the spirit world gave me a healthy viewpoint on the subject.

There is no personal god with a long white beard who sits on a throne issuing orders, the kind of god we are taught from kindergarten to understand. It's more a spark of light within each and every thing, flowers, mankind, animals, in fact anything which lives, a force which touches everything. Every one of us has this force of wonder within our souls, a spark of good, which glows when we decide to give instead of take, love rather than hate, smile rather than scowl, laugh with tears instead of take revenge.

I have watched those in the spirit worlds who hold beliefs in a personal god still stand in awe of a huge cross. They have kept their beliefs intact. I have watched as prayers of hope or want shine like a beam of blue light from the earth to the spirit worlds. Only the prayers of hope arrive at the gates of the spirit realms. The appeals of want make a terrible din and rarely find their way, while the prayers of hope, sounding like beautiful music, win through.

The spirit worlds have a very simple answer on the question of Jesus. He was a teacher who came to teach that period of time and that race of people how to love. This is more difficult than focusing on war and how to kill. It has been revealed to others and me that Jesus was not the first teacher. Many more have entered our lives for the same purpose. Rarely do we notice their presence among us until it's too late.

What I have been taught from the spirits is that we, even on the earth, are working steadily toward our own spiritual paths. Centuries of a good and peaceful way of life will help us all toward joining the godhead. We probably will not achieve it in this lifetime but, if we keep trying, we may realise one day that there is more to life than meets the eye. It is never too late to change our old habits of being thoughtless or uncaring. Then we may stand a chance of doing what a man once tried so hard to teach us about loving one another.

The main purpose of the spirit worlds coming so close to us and delivering messages of hope is to inform us to just simply love and care each other before it's too late. So many people only know how to hurt others, the thought of caring never enters their minds. It has been said that their souls are so thin and withered they cannot expand like other people's souls can. The spirits try to teach us something so powerful, how to tolerate other races and of course our own families, friends and neighbours.

Have you ever boarded a bus to find most seats taken? You peer around, trying to decide which seat to take. You get the feeling that this person nearest is unpleasant, another further down the bus feels friendly, so you move to sit next to them, even though you have to move further into the bus to do so. It is said that this mark on the soul stays until the great return to the spirit realms, unless they work to change their thought pattern.

There appears to be a silver thread of truth running through every religion in every society. They all seem to agree on the same principle that a force much greater than human kind is there ahead of us. I wonder what that force thinks about mankind's efforts for peace and goodwill or even how we treat others on this road back home to the mighty force.

Chapter Six

Physical manifestations

Ten years after I began working with the spirit realms, a change took place in my public hearings. Suddenly spirits began superimposing their faces on the ground in front of me for everyone to see. It is considered a rare medium who has this ability to draw spirit entities more physically forward so they can be heard and seen by a hall full of people. It is normally done only in small organised groups of sympathetic people. But soon my spirits weren't content with producing just faces. Oh no, they had to produce a full-blown show for one audience.

All I had done was give an innocent talk on the Fox sisters, the children responsible for bringing us Spiritualism. The Fox sisters were teenagers in the USA some 150 years ago. They made contact with a deceased peddler who had been buried inside the family home before the family moved there. Knocks and raps from the peddler encouraged the girls to ask questions. A system of communication was developed, much to the delight of the girls. The innocence of these children was the key which led others to begin working with the spirit realms. Spiritualism grew around the world, attracting to it many eminent people. Mediumship itself however is as old as mankind. From the Egyptians and through most religions everywhere in the world, a belief in life after death is rarely questioned, just accepted.

My talk was going well, I thought. Suddenly a lady on the far right of the room began to wave her arms about to attract attention. I stopped speaking and gradually a hushed silence crept over the hall, as more and more of the congregation heard what I could clearly hear. From the back of the hall, spirit children were running towards the stage, a short distance behind me. Invisible feet thumped the floorboards down the sides of the hall, then banged their way noisily up the small steps onto the stage where red velvet curtains were drawn together. One or two tripped. A shoe was stubbed on the steps as they made their way noisily onto the stage. The eyes of everyone in the audience were firmly fixed on this invisible parade of cheeky spirit youngsters. The stage curtains billowed outward as the children raced past... and then silence. In an instant they were all gone.

I took a deep breath and turned to the audience, worried that this spectacle had upset or frightened them. But I needn't have worried, or got so uptight. The congregation loved it; in fact they wanted more, MORE! I nearly cried with disbelief. But instead, I howled with laughter with them. What a night!

To complete the evening, a mother came over to me and took my hand. 'Thank you,' she whispered quietly.

'This evening has put my mind at rest. I lost my darling son a few years ago. Now I know he's all right. I'm sure I heard his voice with those other children, when they ran past.' Her voice filled with emotion. 'Bless you, love, you're special.'

That night was spectacular and fortunately everyone present enjoyed and benefited from the display that the spirit world put on. However, as a responsible person, I felt that others might find this sort of display worrying or even frightening. It wasn't in anybody's interest to alarm anyone. It would only result in worry and pain, not least for me as I would suffer extreme pain in my solar plexus or a feeling of sickness, should someone be alarmed at any of these exercises. I hoped that particular evening would be the last of those kinds of displays but I couldn't risk it happening again, so I decided to retire from that physical side of mediumship.

But there's no stopping the spirit world if they decide I'm to try something new. I do enjoy exploring anything unusual. If someone tells me I must not do something, I go ahead and try it anyway. If I hear of another group or medium starting an unusual task, I like to become involved in its infancy. There are so many areas unexplored. If you try to do something different with the safety of your spirit guide at hand, it can be a fantastic result.

I began to wonder if I could set up a permanent recording link between the two worlds. How the barriers of Heaven could push through the gates of earth if it worked. So I bought a tape recorder and waited until the quiet early hours of the morning to start the experiment.

I placed the recorder on a wooden table, switched the tape on and went to bed. Next morning, full of anticipation, I played the tape back. Dogs barked, a car went by, then absolutely nothing. I realised it would take patience and time but I had both. Every night, I put on fresh tapes and every morning I listened for voices. Nothing, just something known as white noise.

Then, Eureka! The voices of two spirits, albeit very quiet, but voices all the same, encouraging each other to speak.

'Go on, you say it,' said one female voice.

'No! You do it,' said a young man. Then, as if changing their minds together, I could hear, '1,2,3,' in unison then nothing again. This was all I needed. I kept playing my tapes every night, sometimes asking a question first, in the hope of receiving a reply. But not once did I get one. I gave up after a while, believing that, if the spirit realms intended putting their voices on tape, then they would do so with very little help from me.

And of course they did. I always suggest that when people come for a private session, they bring either a new tape or a friend who can record whatever messages come through. When people choose to bring a tape, I ask them to open it and put it in the recorder, then leave them to switch it on. Often, if I touch something electrical, it goes haywire. Anyway, this way, there's no chance of people thinking I've switched the tapes. Soon people started phoning me, telling me their loved ones' voices could be heard on their tapes. Sometimes it was my voice that could be heard, at other times it was a spirit voice or spirit music. What a wonderful thing it was, I thought, when a grieving party could hear their loved ones speaking, clearly and without question, just one more time. Soon, it got so common that I could give a percentage on the chances of this happening, though naturally, no one can guarantee this phenomenon. The most spectacular occurrence was a gentleman whose father spoke into the tape – a father who had passed over to the spirit world some five years before.

The slurred elderly voice filled the room.

'Is that you, Frances?' John Castagna replayed the tape and again the voice spoke strongly, repeating the same question.

'That's definitely my father's voice,' John said quietly.

I sat stunned. John had brought this tape, then new and unwrapped, to a sitting a few days before.

He and his wife (they are now divorced) came for a private sitting after attending a spiritualist church service. John filled me in on the background to his decision to visit me. He had been born in Australia but his parents who were Maltese moved back to Malta when he was three. In 1970, his mother decided to move to Wales as her father had been Welsh, and John, then 17, came with her.

The small family settled down, only disturbed occasionally by the 'things' John's mother used to see. Occasionally she'd be talking to herself in the bathroom and then would tell her sister the 'big one' wanted to talk to her. She worked in a shopping centre in Newport with John's wife; in fact the two had become really friendly. Often in work, John's mother saw a little girl walking towards her, though no one else seemed to see her. John told me that he learnt later that the shopping centre had been built over a cemetery.

Life carried on, then in 1988, John's father died after suffering a series of strokes which had left his speech distorted. But it was only after his mother died in 1994 that John went to the spiritualist meeting to get in touch with his parents but failed. I don't have time at services to speak to everyone in the audience so personal sittings are often best if people are desperate to contact loved ones. Once John had filled in the background, I asked him to position the recorder, insert the tape and switch it on. The room got very cold, then someone called Charles told me he'd come to talk to John. John identified Charles as his father. Then his mother came too. After identifying herself to me, she said the strangest thing.

'Frances, this'll prove it to him. Tell him I keep cheese in my handbag.' I laughed.

'Why on earth?'
'Go on, just tell him.' I passed it on as instructed. John looked bewildered.

'No-one keeps cheese in their bag. Chocolate maybe, cheese, no.' I shrugged my shoulders, about to explain I was only the messenger, when John's wife spoke up for the first time.

'But she did.' John was completely shocked.
'You're joking. How on earth do you know that?'
'I worked alongside her for years, remember. It's amazing how well you get to know

people in those sorts of situations. It's not so surprising that I knew. But how on earth did Frances know?' They both turned to look at me.

'I just pass on what people say to me,' I explained weakly, though even I was slightly taken aback. Queerer things were to happen. John went straight to work after we finished the sitting, leaving his wife to take the tapes and recorder home. I thought nothing of it, until I got a phone call from John the following morning.

'When I got back from work last night,' he said in a strange voice. 'Maria was sitting shaking. She'd played the tapes and recognised my father's voice on them.'

For a moment, I sat there. I could hardly believe what he was telling me. Quickly we arranged for him to bring the tapes round to me, so I could hear them for myself.

I could hardly contain myself until he arrived about an hour later. Agonisingly slowly, he set up the recorder again and inserted the tape. The quality wasn't bad, though as always my voice seems to be at some distance away. Then suddenly, much closer to the microphone came another slurred voice with a foreign accent.

'Is that you, Frances?'
I remembered, at the start of the sitting, the spirit who'd said he was Charles asking that question. The spirits I hear in my inner ear - clairaudience - are clear and speak in their earthly voices, but of course they can't be heard in the room. They give me messages to pass on to my client. This phenomenon, of a spirit voice actually recording onto tape, is called Electrical Voice Phenomenon and is very rare.

But was John absolutely sure it was his father's voice?
'Oh yes,' said John. 'Of course I recognise it and so did Maria. He spoke in that slurred way at the end of his life because of his strokes. He sounds so close, much closer than your voice. Anyway, even if it wasn't him - and I'm certain it is him - whose voice is it and where did it come from? What's it doing on my tape?'

I have to take John's word that the voice on the tape is his father's, just as I had to take the spirit's word that he was Charles. All I can say with certainty is that the voice on the tape is the voice I heard at the time spiritside. I just never expected it to record onto tape.

It is my personal belief that if the spirit realms have a procedure which they feel will work, then I am happy to try it. If it should fail, then no tears are shed, we try something else instead. The only thing I demand is I must be wide-awake. I do not relish the thought of being asleep while everyone else is having all the fun.

Yet another remarkable phenomenon was in store for my clients. The spirits chose to physically be felt in a private sitting. Though I could never guarantee that this would happen, sittings became interactive in all sorts of ways. Many clients enjoyed embraces, kisses and hugs with those who had passed over to the spirit realms, holding a loved one just one more time before they stepped back behind the invisible curtain to the Summerland. Spirit children played happily in their parents' presence once more or sat on the knees of their mums or dads.

This practice needs careful handling. I make sure my client is happy for this to happen, then I insist on confirmation that the spirit is actually who it says it is. Only then am I happy for the spirit guides to let the spirit loved one move forward to embrace the waiting relative. Some overzealous spirit family members can be a little too quick and are hugging before they have permission, swooping an arm around a loved one while that loved one was still deciding whether to allow it or not. But I've never known anyone to be angry or upset by this.

I had known Christine from my workdays at the local hospital. We became great friends very quickly. One day over a cup of coffee in a local cafe Christine asked me casually what happened to babies and little children when they go over. I thought it was just a casual enquiry so explained, using fictitious names to illustrate a situation of mother and new baby.

'The baby is normally accompanied by a special soul, one that may have known the mother through the bloodline. Let's take for example a baby I'll call Robert who happened to have passed over say a year ago.'

Christine's eyes grew large and her mouth dropped.

'I called my baby Robert,' she explained tearfully. 'He died a year ago.' I sat there stunned, wishing the floor would swallow me up.

'Christine, I am so sorry. I had absolutely no idea you'd ever had a child, let alone that he had died. If I'd known you were grieving so, I'd have approached this so differently. Let me help you.

Come to my house for a sitting and let's see if Robert comes through. Or maybe we can learn something about him from other spirits. Would that help?' Christine nodded, drying her eyes.

'Sorry to be so weepy, you'd think I'd be getting over it a bit by now. But I'd like to try and find out how he is, if you think you can.'

'We'll try everything we can,' I promised her. 'Make sure you bring a new tape with you, so that you'll be able to listen to it again if we get any information.'

A few days later, Christine turned up, bringing her own mother with her to hold her hand. The first person through was Christine's mother's mother, who told me that she and a few others were taking great care of Robert. Tears flowed, as did laughter as her grandmother recounted recent episodes from Robert's spirit life.

'Enjoy your tape, my dear,' said her grandmother gently, just before she drifted away. 'Remember, Robert is very much at home here, he is happy. Remember he is happy.'

The phone rang loudly that afternoon. Christine sounded quite different, relaxed, as if she was beginning to come to terms with her loss.

' Frances, you'll never guess what. I can't thank you enough. It's amazing, absolutely amazing. You wait till you hear it, I'll never forget today.' Trying to get a word in was more than difficult, she was so excited.

'Christine, wait, wait. Just what has happened? What are you talking about?'

'Didn't I say? Oh, I'm so stupid, but I'm just so happy and excited. I heard Robert's voice on the tape. He cried a little then laughed. It was so amazing, I can't thank you enough. I know my baby is all right now and I can get on with my life.' At that moment I heard another voice, a spirit voice. It was the grandmother.

'Tell her she will hear the voice one more time before it fades.'
'Why does it have to fade? It's bringing Christine such joy,' I protested.

'We know that but Robert is not strong enough or old enough to penetrate the tape permanently, so it will fade. But at least she knows that he is well and happy.'

Distressed though she was to hear the tape wasn't permanent, Christine used the knowledge to call all the family together so they could all hear the tape of her baby for the one and only time.

Everyone agreed it was wonderful and that Robert sounded just like her other children. He was never again heard on that tape which faded just like the grandmother had said it would.

Christine has managed to get on with her life, secure in the knowledge that her son is being cared for and loved by members of her family and that one day in the future they will be in each other's arms once again, this time forever.

I would not break a trust and can't divulge all the contents of the sittings, but those I have mentioned were very special sittings. Some people were so sad, and then so happy, after their loved ones brought blessings of love. I was once asked if spirits talk of love and gush flowery words all over the place. Many people think that when a loved one draws close, they are only capable of whispering words of love. Personally I have found this not to be true as often loved ones will tell off the recipient of the message, especially if they feel it's necessary. A parent or spouse will be cross if they think their relative has gone wrong or if they think their lives have been broken down by grief. Some may even cuss a little, although that's rarer.

Chapter Seven

Immediate communication

One of the saddest passing's is one where we have failed to say goodbye, or maybe we have argued and then not had the opportunity to say sorry before that special person passes to the higher life. Filled with despair, we grow more and more angry and grief-stricken, sometimes taking to drink or other escape routes to hide away from the guilt and anger. Yet the best thing we could do after the trauma of losing a loved one - scream, rant and rage – is the one thing we try hard not to do. Our souls are crying out for that special person and such release can be part and parcel of the healing process.

What we don't realise is that all the time our loved ones in the spirit world see this problem. They try to reach out to us but we take no notice, believing them gone forever with no communication possible. Yet our loved ones can read all our thoughts, even the ones we try to hide. They are able to see how sorry we are. They know how pride prevented us from just whispering 'I'm sorry' or 'I really do love you. Will you ever forgive me?' The last thing a loved one wants to do is leave us with sorrow. So they make every effort to come closer to us and let us know that everything is all right. They want to tell us they have moved on and are making headway in their new life.

Once I started working regularly as a medium, I began to notice how often spirits returned very soon after their departure to the spirit realms. I started wondering how many people had experienced communication from their loved ones during these early days, so I carried out some research, backing it up with information from my clients. It soon became very evident that spirits do return to earth within the first three weeks of departure, usually to inform their loved ones that they are settled in their new world. It is normal for them to return again and again until the grieving ones manage to deal with the shock and loss. I have also been told that the spirit will then move onto other planes of existence, as slowly and surely they move back and become part of the community they are meant to be with.

If a loved one who has departed from you needs to get through to you, they will break through in any manner they can. Dreams can be a wonderful source of communication though this usually only happens with family or close friends. So many times widows or widowers have described how they have felt a partner lying in bed next to them, long after they have gone to the New World. Those left behind often say they try not to breathe in case 'they go again'. This seems to be a common emotion experienced by all those to whom this happens.

The presence of a departed loved one can often be deduced if a series of items like earrings, cufflinks, photos go missing within the home. Blame it on your loved ones. John Redmond explained to me that loved ones in the spirit world often return for a brief visit, just to pick up items as a keepsake in their new life. Occasionally the same person who originally borrowed them returns these items.

I'm sure many people 'feel' the presence of a loved one within the family home, but then wonder if they can be seen by the spirit while they are in the bathroom or attending to more private functions. Let me put your mind at rest straightaway. If a spirit, any spirit, is found snooping around your private life, that spirit has broken a natural law of privacy and would be punished. Of course, if you invite them in to enjoy again their presence, that's quite different but you would have to agree to this beforehand. Only when a spirit is attempting to get your attention in the middle of the night should you tell it firmly to 'get lost'. You have all day for chatting or going for walks. You need your rest for your well being. I certainly would not waken from a good night's sleep to pander to the whims of anyone, never mind the spirit world!

Some people worry that if they move house, their spirit loved ones would get left behind. Again, you don't need to worry about that. Loved ones know when such events are about to take place and there is no reason why they can't go along with you. It would not surprise me if they didn't have some sort of opinion about the new property that you have chosen to buy. But just remember that it's you who will be living in that house so choose wisely.

It was while I was preparing my private survey on whether spirits remain in the vicinity of loved ones for a while after passing that a personal tragedy happened to my family and me. The very sudden passing of a favourite cousin took everyone by surprise. No one had expected him to die so young. He had suffered from a mental illness which is one of life's miseries from beginning to end for everyone concerned. Thank goodness he returned to me immediately.

Instead of his ruffled appearance in life, my cousin looked smart and well groomed, his hair styled and managed. His face was no longer tormented but filled with the relaxed smile of one who had found his peace. He told me that, after his sudden departure from this world, he walked into the arms of those who shone a golden light which reached far across the riverbank where death stalked his footsteps. He walked into the arms of people who willed him to everlasting peace and took him to the safety of a land far more beautiful and gentle than this world. I also learnt that his mental illness left him at the moment of his death. From his rest my cousin was greeted by those he remembered from the years before illness took its painful and tormenting grip on his life. Because of his mental problems, he had never been allowed to drive on this earth, but he excitedly told me he had been given permission to drive the largest train in the heavens. Trains had been a passion from his childhood and now he was going to travel the heavens in style, carrying passengers along at great speeds.

I have known of other people's deceased loved ones wanting to extend their thanks to a particular person. Often this person has turned out to be the Funeral Director. They explain to their startled and grieving families that a thank you card would be nice for Mr So and so. 'He did treat me so well, and with such dignity, before my big day.' (The funeral).

This happened to another young lady whose father was in the spirit world, though it took him ten years to find a way through. He asked her through me if she could send his thanks to the undertaker for the wonderful way in which he had been treated with dignity and respect. At least this proves they don't forget a kindness shown. God bless 'em.

Often a loved one makes a comment on their forthcoming funeral. I helped a young wife whose husband fell victim to a particularly nasty condition known as Huntingdon's Chorea. She first came to me over twenty-five years ago when her husband first started deteriorating. By now, she had to be both mum and dad to their children and had no one to turn to when the going got rough. Often she would turn up unexpectedly on my doorstep and together we would listen while members of the family, already in the spirit world, such as her late father and her first child, came through with advice. They helped her with all sorts of problems, from handling the children as they grew up into teenagers to boosting her confidence when she was depleted from running around after her very sick husband, as mentally and physically he deteriorated, looking more like a seventy-year-old man than a young 30-year-old.

When he became too ill for her to handle, he was taken into hospital. For several years he lay there, unable to do anything for himself. For some time, husband and wife were able to be together when she visited but then he lost the ability to recognise her or the children any longer.

His painful death, despite being a release for him, became such a grief for the little family. A few days later, they arrived at my home, hoping he would come through with his choice of hymns for his funeral. Not only did he come through, but explained in detail the life he was now living.

'Darling, it's wonderful here,' he announced. 'I don't have to lie around while others feed me. I can walk, talk, and move. I can eat and, my darling, I am well.' An air of sadness wafted around us as he quietly spoke to his young wife. 'If only we could have had a better life than the one we had.' His voice trailed off as his wife picked up his mood.

'We were together and that's what counts,' she said bravely. 'What hymns do you want? Have we chosen the right ones for you? Do you like them?'

'No!' came the giggly response. 'They are miserable. I am happy. Can I have a Tina Turner record?'

Stunned, his wife inquired how he knew of Tina Turner and her records, as she hadn't been as famous when her husband had been well enough to be aware of such things.

'Simple,' he replied with a grin, 'I could hear you humming to her records this morning on the radio. At home. I was there.'

He got his wish. The funeral was quiet, not many turned up. He had lost touch with all his friends many years before. But his family were there and that's what counts. I don't see his wife now she has moved on but at least she had a shoulder to cry on when it was needed.

My family and friends used to meet once a week to play bingo at our local community hall. Gradually Nancy became part of our group. Her sister Joan was already something of a regular with us, joining in with all the jokes and memories we shared over those few hours. All Nancy told us about herself was that she had looked after the two sisters' ageing mother. She was a pleasant woman who seemed quite shy compared sister Joan. A little older and more elegant in her dress sense, Nancy did not wear a wedding ring so I thought she had never married, staying at home to take care of mum.

One week, as usual we gathered together on Wednesday, recounting the week's events to one another as we enjoyed the bingo games. Next morning my eyes nearly fell out of my head, for in my kitchen standing as bold as brass was Nancy.

'How did you get in here?' I asked. 'How did you know where I lived?' But Nancy took no notice of my queries.

'Tell Joan I'm with John,' she said, smiling as she began to fade away in front of my eyes. As she spoke I realised she was a spirit and I snatched the opportunity to ask if she had gone down there first, indicating with my finger Hell. My answer was a reassuring smile.

'No, there was no need for me to go through all that.' Then she faded away.

I slumped into a nearby chair, convinced I had never given my address to Nancy. And I certainly had never informed her of my spiritual work or that I was a medium. So how on earth had she found out she could speak to me in her spiritual voice?

I looked at the clock, it was 8.30 am. Slowly I rose from my chair and prepared to go shopping. As I entered the first shop, I spotted Joan, Nancy's sister. I called to her and she turned and walked slowly over to me.

'Frances.' She could hardly speak for tears. Large dark circles under her eyes told their own story. She clutched a sodden white handkerchief in her hand and kept dabbing at her swollen face. 'Our Nancy died last night just after midnight. It was so sudden. She wasn't even ill. It was a blood clot on the brain. Will you tell your mum?' I nodded, mumbling how sorry I was.

This was not the time to tell Joan that her recently departed sister was in my home, giving me a message for her. It would have to wait for a more suitable time and place. I recalled that Nancy had told me that she was with

John. I wondered who John was. Later on that day, when I looked in the local newspaper, I found out. The deaths column stated clearly:

Nancy reunited with late husband John.

The years have rolled on and I don't see Joan any more. I never found myself in a position to be able to pass on the message Nancy brought that morning. No matter what messages come to me from the spirit lands, I will not pass them on to living relatives or friends, unless that person comes to me to try to contact the deceased. It is not for me to intrude on another's grief, they have to find their own time and place to come to me when they are prepared to contact the spirit world. Often of course the spirit nudges their relative or friend in my direction and then I am only too happy to pass on whatever messages come my way.

This happened in a private reading for a young granddaughter of an old client of mine, a month after the elderly lady's demise. The family had sought out a clairvoyant to see if the old lady was all right after her funeral as naturally they were still grieving. To the clairvoyant's surprise and the family's, the old lady refused to speak to the clairvoyant. All she would say was 'I want to speak to FRANCES.' The family looked at one another for clues as to who this Frances could be. No one in their family was called Frances, so who could he or she be?

A few days went by and the elder of the family returned to the old lady's flat. Wandering around picking up bits and pieces, he came across an address book, with my telephone number in it. The family booked an appointment and my client, the old lady, came through with tons of information for them all, at the same time telling them off gently for not coming earlier.

A more sombre use of this power to contact spirits shortly after their departure has been in connection with those who suffer untimely deaths. The mother of one murder victim came to see me to ask if I could help catch her daughter's killer. Her daughter came through to me immediately but could hardly speak. I managed to make out the words 'Rob' and 'Photo'. I wondered if the girl had been killed during the course of a robbery. It turned out later, when the police caught the killer, that his name was Robinson and he featured on a family photograph, as he had once been a friend of the girl he had killed. The police were naturally very sceptical the first time I went to them with some information relating to a murder. I got the usual sly laughs and knowing looks but I persevered, convinced that I was right. They were forced to listen to me when, several months later, they arrested the killer exactly where I'd said he'd be. They agreed to send two policemen round to talk to me. They did the usual 'good cop, bad cop' routine, where one appeared to be very friendly and believed in me, while the other refused to believe anything I had to say and seemed to just want to leave the house. But I had help they just didn't know about. The father of one of them came through and gave me his son's nickname at the station and some personal details about both of them. When I told them this, their jaws just hit the ground. I had to laugh quietly to myself, particularly when they told me that in fact the one who'd been giving me a hard time was in fact a believer, while the so-called 'believer' had been totally sceptical. Both left my house converted to believing that somehow I 'knew' things. Since then, they keep in regular contact and I have helped them on a number of occasions.

A British girl, on holiday in France with her husband, went missing. The French police, through her husband, asked for my help. I could see fields and a long line of trees, a signpost, and a low wall. They eventually found a shoe near a signpost and her body in a wood.

Obviously this sort of work can be unpleasant, especially when you are able to see murder victims and talk to them. Some of them are so confused and can't understand what has happened to them or why. I see my job as reassuring them as well as those left behind.

Chapter Eight

Danger

Countless occasions in the past three decades have brought accounts of Spirits and the Dark Side. A door to the unknown has been pushed open by inquiring minds nervously exploring behind the veil of life. Now, they have been publicly thrown open for debate and newspaper reporting. Instances of appalling, and degrading behaviour by unknown and frightening creatures of the darkness, forever challenging to the human race, have brought what was obviously needed for their presence in our World, a destruction of emotion to terrifyingly cold fear, shrilled cries echo from a short distance just in earshot.

From psychic fire starters to haunting visitations, I have moved from one breathtaking moment to the next, my only weapon was my belief and trust in those I had formed a close trusting friendship with, my spiritual companions.

When I hear about families experiencing problems with a haunting, I go into my rebellious mode. I am so angry and have such a need to sort it out that my spouse says my back legs buzz like a cricket's, in anticipation of what's in store! I come across it only a few times a year. Usually all that's happening is that loved ones from the spirit world are making a mess of contacting their families. Spirits have many ways of saying "It's me, love, I just dropped in to say hello" but sometimes all they manage to accomplish is havoc. They try so hard but only move pictures or knock photos off shelves which ends up terrifying instead of comforting those left behind.

But occasionally a haunting is far more serious. One thing I hadn't contemplated was getting involved in a fight with the darker side. Well, I didn't do the fighting, the spirit world did, though it was held in my home. Normally a safe refuge from anyone or thing with thoughts to harm or penetrate our treasured existence.

Protectively in the white corner - my dearest friends in the spirit realms.

And in the black corner, a voodoo witch in a spiritual body.

Thankfully the whole family was out at work or school. I'd been the last to leave, closing the living room door as I left for work, to stop our two young pups from wandering the house and getting into trouble. At twelve o'clock my son arrived at work to get me, saying he'd just come home to find the fire brigade and police sifting through the remains of the living room, which had been totally gutted by fire. When I walked in, I gazed in horror at the state of the room. Everything had been thrown around. Irreplaceable photos and personal items were tossed everywhere, although I'd carefully kept them in folders inside my sideboard. But one item remained totally unscathed - a perfect silk rose which had been given to me at a church where I'd held a particularly successful service. The only other relatively undamaged item in the room was a large silver cross which my father had given me and which my local parish priest had blessed. It was bent and twisted and had started to melt, and somehow it had become embedded upside down in the video player, but at least it was still very recognisable. Later, when we sorted through all the debris, I came across another undamaged item - a psychic picture of Che Fu Yeng, which had been drawn for me by a medium. Strangest of all, the firemen found the pups upstairs under my bed, fine except for needing a puff of oxygen and none the worse after their terrifying experience. So who opened the living room door for them to escape the fire?

The firemen told me the fire, which had caused over £10,000's worth of damage, had apparently begun some two hours after I had left the house, though they couldn't explain how it had started. Neither could they explain the ransacking of a room which I had left in perfect order that morning. But I could - I knew exactly what had happened.

The day before, I'd had a visit from a young man who'd come to see me privately. As he sat down, one of my cats jumped up onto his lap and started snuffling around. I could hardly believe my eyes - this cat was so frightened of people he never went to anyone. Then I saw a ghostly hand coming out from the young man's open-necked shirt, through his breastbone. It seemed to be searching for something.

'Dear God,' I thought, 'What's that?'

Suddenly the cat seemed to see it too and, with outstretched claws, pounced up onto the hand, tearing the young man's chest so badly that blood poured everywhere. The hand disappeared and the cat, losing interest, jumped off his lap and wandered over to a sunny patch by the window.

Catching my breath, I handed my visitor some tissues, apologising for the cat's strange behaviour. As he mopped himself, I waited for the next move. It was only a matter of seconds before I heard a spirit tell me that my visitor's mother was trying to use her son for her own ends and was tormenting him.

'I think this is something to do with your mother, isn't it?' I asked gently. He stopped the mopping and looked at me, stunned.

'They said you were good but that's amazing. How on earth can you possibly know that?' I smiled and waited. Gradually, he told me his story. His deceased mother, a Voodoo priestess, had ordered him to get involved with spiritualism, telling him that great things would come of it if he did. She had frightened him into believing that she held a spell over him, which could not be broken by any means. I disagreed and told him that his mother would not have dominance over me or him, as the power of the spirit was, and always would be, far stronger.

'Give up any thoughts of spiritualism,' I advised, as I waved him goodbye. That's an end to that, I thought.

How wrong could I be? Over the next fourteen hours, all hell was let loose. The spiritual entity which was his mother obviously remained in my house, furious with what I had told her son. Luckily for us, I had friends in high places, (forgive the pun) and they saved our family from what would definitely have been certain death. They fought to hold back that fire for those crucial hours, so that the house was vacant when the room burst into flames, destroying a home carefully built up over the years. If the Voodoo priestess had had her way, we'd all have died in that fire.

Stranger things were yet to come. Some hours after the fire had been put out, Keith took some photos of the room before it was demolished. We couldn't believe our eyes when we had the photos developed. Many of the pictures showed the fire still raging on, hours after it had been extinguished. The developed photos show, extremely clearly, flames licking up the window where once my curtains hung. We showed the photographs to a photographic lecturer who concluded they were ghost photographs. I can only conclude that the fire and the fight were still being fought to the brink in the spirit world, well after we thought it was over.

It is comforting to know that if you help the spirits, they in return will guard us to the bitter end, and fight like terriers for our well being. Now we can laugh at the way we had to manage our lives after the fire. We had to live upstairs in the bedrooms, while the downstairs was being renewed. As it was so near Christmas, we were forced to make do the best we could. That year we decorated our Christmas tree on the landing, which even today never fails to reduce us to tears of laughter. To add insult to injury, before the fire we had taken in a lodger, as he had nowhere to live, and so he too had to make do.

In my quieter moments, and after some very scant information from a person who thought he was very knowledgeable on spiritual matters, I realised that the protection afforded by the spirit guides would see me out of any scrape I found myself in. Being me, I thought I would try out this newfound protection so I stood in the middle of the road while a lorry thundered toward me. But I didn't wait around long enough to find out if it worked, I dived for cover, and realised just what protection meant. It was of course of the spiritual type, which I would need plenty of later on when things got even more hairy.

Mediumship is not all roses and I was soon to find out that not every spirit is as cheerful as the many thousands that I had been privileged to speak to.

The Christmas period is a time for enjoying one another's company. Friends old and new drop in to the home to be warmed by a glass of mulled wine and a medieval Christmas mince pie. Conversation stays light, and laughter abounds. Of course when you have a family as large as we, seventeen at the last count, there is a great deal of preparation for the big event. Trimming the home takes precedence over everything and the smell of fruits, nuts and other delicacies permeate the whole home.

It had been a particularly good Christmas Day that year. Nevertheless a Boxing Day of sport and old films was a welcome relief from feeding people who seemed forever hungry. It's always a pleasure to have our children and their children around us, we love them all, but we're so glad when they go home to their own homes. It's a chance to collapse in the biggest chair available, which was at last empty of children opening yet more gifts.

Keith had gone down to the local to meet up with his friends. I was alone in the house, enjoying the well-earned peace when the phone rang about 5pm that evening. As I walked over to the phone, my stomach began to turn over, a sure sign that the spirit world had broken away from their festivals in the heavens to attend to worldly needs.

'Hello?' I enquired lightly, knowing this was not a 'wish you a merry Christmas call'. A man's voice, serious and strong, asked if I was the Frances Powles the medium.

'I am,' I answered, 'How can I help you?' Still my stomach turned somersaults of their own accord.

'Your name was given to me by another medium, and he suggested I ring you.' The man's voice was cautious.

'I won't be working until after the New Year,' I interrupted.
'I hoped you might be able to help us before then, we're desperate,' he argued, concerned. He didn't wait for my response but carried on explaining. 'My wife and I are having problems. Even the priest has blessed the house, but it has not stopped the problem.' Oh, great, I thought, that's all I need even before the New Year's bells were rung. I asked his name.

'Vince,' he replied. 'Vincent Brown. My wife's name is Lisa. Can you come to our home?' How could I refuse? If there's one thing to get my blood boiling, it's a lonesome spook trying to cause problems for our young folk.

'What time can you pick me up?' I asked Vince.
'How about the next few minutes? We're staying with relatives until this is cleared up, they live close to you.'

I left my family a note, giving the name, address and telephone number I could be reached at, and explained briefly where and what I was doing. I could imagine how thrilled they were going to be. After all I had promised that I would not work over the festive season. Oh well you can't help emergencies.

The car screeched to a halt outside my home. Inside the car were Vince, Lisa, and two or three family members. The look of concern on their faces convinced me they were suffering untold problems. I introduced myself and we set off to the Brown's home a few miles away. The family filled me in on what had upset their Christmas Festivities.

My initial thoughts as always were to wonder who'd been playing with an Ouija board. I often wonder why people think that the festive season is a time to lark around with these unknown elements. I must admit, however, that I too thought when I was much younger that it was fun to make an Ouija board of our own in a Wimpy bar in town.

That is until it shot off the brown laminate table with an empty glass in tow. I was first out of that cafe, leaving my friends to explain to the manageress what we had been doing. I thought she would blow a fuse, but she was disgusted that we had not called her over to join in - she loved things like that. However, the young couple who drove me to their home that evening had not been so foolish as to try anything this silly. So I would have to look elsewhere for the source of the problem.

Time was getting on by the time we reached the Browns family home. It was quite dark outside, and the air was chilly but clear. We all got out of the car and while the family entered the house I studied it for a while outside. I was looking to spot weaknesses around the home. It always has a lopsided view to me when something is spiritually wrong. The house had been built only a few years ago on wasteland, Vince informed me before we went inside to join Lisa and the rest of the family in a pot of tea to warm against the cold night. Always wise to go in twos anywhere where it's a bit on edge.

I felt nothing as I entered the downstairs hall and the rest of the down-stairs rooms. However, an overwhelming urge to charge upstairs came over me. I'd never experienced anything like this feeling before.

'You must need a lot of help,' I whispered to anyone from the other side of life who might have been listening. No one answered. 'Do you mind if I wander around to get the feel of the place?' I asked Lisa.

'No, no, carry on, do what you have to,' she urged, smiling awkwardly. 'I need to go upstairs first,' I explained. 'I feel compelled to check something out.' Nobody said anything, then the family burst into conversation again, trying to appear as if they weren't in the least bit worried. As Vince and I walked into the hall, I blanked them out of my mind and attempted contact mentally with whatever spirits, good or bad, may have been around. The hall stairs ran up the left-hand side of the house. There was a sense of newness about the property. There was also a sense of someone on the landing. I knew it couldn't be any of the family, they were all in the downstairs lounge. My heart began to pound a little as I climbed the stairs. Vince followed me, explaining what had happened over the Christmas period.

'I saw a little boy. He came into the bedroom as if he was playing. I thought it was odd and asked him where he had come from but he didn't answer me or even seem to hear me at all. He just threw a hat at me, then ran out and vanished. It happened several times more until we couldn't stand it anymore. That's when we moved out.'

'Have you been back since?'

'We came back when the priest came to bless the house. That was my mother's idea. She suggested we contact the Church and fair play, he was great and came out straightaway but when we moved back in afterwards, the same thing started happening all over again, only worse. So we moved out again.'

'Why don't you go down and sit with your wife?' I suggested. 'Keep everyone in the front room. I'll go on and see what's there.' Thankfully Vince ignored me and carried on climbing the stairs. I don't mind telling you I was scared to bits, but it's no good letting that side of me show. After all I was a medium, and mediums don't get scared, do they? No, I told myself, and I'm not going to let anything scare me.

'Come on, Vince,' I said aloud, to give me confidence as much as anything. 'Let's sort this out.'

Following the stairs around a curve, which led to the top of the landing, Vince pointed out his bedroom and their baby's room next door. But it was the front bedroom, which stored everything from a cot to unused carpets, which was calling me. That was the room I felt carried a problem - the spiritual kind.

'Sorry. There's no light in here,' explained Vince, staying well back from the door into the room. 'Are you going to be all right? Do you want anything?'

'Just water, please.' When my throat dries up, it's always a sign that spirit activity is about to happen. In a second Vince returned with a glass of ice-cold water.

'Do you want me to stay or would you rather be alone?'

'You go on downstairs,' I advised calmly. 'Tell everyone to stay together in the lounge so if I hear a noise I won't mistake it for one of them.' Vince smiled and quietly returned to his family.

The room seemed small, so many new houses do today. As I sat down on a bench behind the bedroom door and opposite the window, I noticed how cold it had become. Grey mists began forming around me, which appeared to grow bigger, almost trying to float into my face. I called Sixpence a spirit child and helper, hoping she would explain what was happening to this house. Something was. It felt uneasily quiet as if several unseen people were watching me. Strangely, I could hear no sounds from downstairs, yet there were at least five people down there, including a toddler. How could they all be so quiet, I wondered. I felt isolated. That was exactly what a troublesome spirit needs me to feel. Shrugging my shoulders, I stood up from the seat in the small bedroom and began to walk around the room. Each step made my stomach turn over. This was silly, I decided.

'Nothing is in this room, or the house for that matter,' I said loudly. Taking sips from the cold glass, I felt the air around me grow even colder. I could see my breath in the darkness of the room against the light pouring in from the landing. Because the room wasn't large, I thought I would immediately feel anyone who stepped close to me. Tingles ran down my neck and left side.

'Hello,' I called out, attempting to encourage communication. Nothing. Silence. I heard Vince racing upstairs again.

'Are you all right?' he asked concerned.
'Yes, love, I'm trying to get someone to talk to me and tell me what's happening,' I explained. Vince shivered.

'Hasn't it gone cold up here?' he remarked.
'Go back down to Lisa,' I said gently. When Vince went downstairs a strange thing happened. I felt completely isolated, as if I had been cut off from everyone else in the house again. It was obviously an attempt to frighten me. I called yet no one heard me. My voice echoed around the top of the house and didn't seem to reach downstairs. How on earth could they not hear me? I asked myself. I walked back onto the landing and leant over the stairs banister, directing my voice toward the bottom half of the house. Once, twice I yelled out. Where were they all? Couldn't they hear me calling? Had they gone outside and not told me, leaving me to deal with this myself? Oh, God I was scared.

I realised it could be a ploy to make me feel that I should run out of the house, so instead I did the opposite. I determined that I was going to get on with the job even if I had no other human contact. At that point I was aware of voices again from downstairs. I could feel the smug look on my face, even if it was only for 'them'. Their efforts to frighten me and make me run were not working. I wet my fingertip, and stroked it in the air. One for Frances, I chuckled. It will take more than turning off the audio sound to the world to frighten me, I whispered through my teeth at anything watching.

Obviously that upset whatever was making this into such a haunted house. Suddenly the whole house plunged into thick darkness, which slid over my face like a rough hand. My mouth filled up with the dense fog like blackness. I stumbled backwards into nothingness, reaching out for a wall or door to save my balance. Stretching out, I fought with the darkness, but it was like fighting rolls of cotton wool. I gathered my mental strength together and refused to accept that this could be possible. Suddenly I could feel the banister beneath my hand. Shockingly a fire alarm above my head screamed off, the siren deafened me. It echoed as if the house was empty of people and furniture. Then as quickly as it all began, it stopped. A hushed unnatural silence descended over the house. A sense of foreboding crept in, in place of the siren, making me feel unsure of myself. If that was the intention, whatever was creating this horror had almost won but again my anger rose up, restoring my courage.

'How dare you!' I hissed into the air. 'How dare you try and frighten me! Who in God's name do you think you are? If you think for one moment you have brought me to my knees, think again. Better than you have tried.'

Now the fight was on. I could feel the tension rising in the air.
'I'm ready for you. Give it your best because you're going back where you came from, and you're going soon,' I declared. There was some noise, and a clap of what sounded like thunder. Then, silence once again, much to my dismay. I heard the family downstairs racing out of the lounge into the hall.

'What happened? Are you all right?' Their voices were clear as their questions travelled up the staircase. Thank goodness, I thought, maybe things will get back to normal now. But of course that would be too much to expect. I shouted down for everyone to remain together and within the room below me. Moments later, the house was again soaked in an unnatural darkness. The smoke alarm flashed on and off, then plunging into loud screeching. On, off, on, off, there was no pattern, just frantic alarm and then prolonged darkness. No one spoke, no one dared. Someone shone a torch into the electric box.

'The alarm isn't fixed up to the electric.' The fear in the voice was evident. 'How did it go off on its own?' Little tingles rolled up and down my neck and through my hair. I was frozen to the bone. My heart and stomach turned over together. I'm not afraid to say that I didn't touch the banister in front of me, just in case a hand came over mine. Instead I pushed my hands into my coat pockets. Panting nervously and aware of threatening eyes surrounding me, I welcomed the anger surging up inside me. I was not going to be reduced to a mumbling wreck. I came to do a job and I was going to complete it.

Again I sent the family back downstairs. Then to my astonishment and utter amazement, the opposite of what had previously occurred unfolded before my eyes. An atmosphere of warmth and love reached out to me, wrapped me in a shawl of security. Help was at hand. I had not been abandoned or ignored, which I'd begun to think was more than a possibility. In the corner of my eye was the most beautiful sight ever to reach my eyes. Sixpence, along with some of the biggest men I have ever seen in my life, was struggling with something I couldn't see. The family and I were safe. Help had arrived. These angels of mercy were there, just as I was, to fight for the good and well being of everyone in that home that night.

Suddenly, my senses were again alerted. Out of the corner of my eye, I could see a glowing light coming from the front bedroom, where I was sitting moments before. It appeared to be daylight but how could it be? It had been dark when I arrived less than an hour before. The light became intense. I felt myself being drawn towards this new phenomenon. Despite its brightness, it didn't make me blink. I drew my eyes away and back to the darkness around me, which now seemed to be friendly and no longer foreboding. The angels of mercy had obviously won that battle.

At the other end of the landing Sixpence was still busy clearing away the dense fog and the energies of those who had came to frighten the family downstairs. For a little one she sure knew her stuff. Working continuously, she sent the negative energy spinning out into the night, through the bathroom window. Smiling she waved at me and vanished.

Now what was in store for me? What else could happen in this house of fear? I had learned long ago not to show or feel fear. It is a food to low life but they were not going to feed off me. Whatever this house called up next, I was tired but ready.

I stood with my back to the bathroom. I needed to concentrate fully on whatever came through the bedroom door next. The light grew stronger. The door and wall melted into a vision which grew before my eyes, a vision of a garden so beautiful, so bright that I was hypnotised by its perfect splendour. Not a December night, cold and unwelcoming, but a summer's day bright with flowers. A pathway led not into the garden. I shook my head. No, I wasn't dreaming. The path led up to an arch, adorned with full red roses cascading down and flowing around hundreds of other flowers. Above the archway the sky was blue and a most incredible feeling of peace flowed outwards from this wonderful and typical English garden.

My eyes barely getting used to this awesome sight, I was slightly alarmed at the figure who emerged slowly from the garden. An old man bent with age glided up to me and settled about two yards away. He raised his arm for my attention but I stood back without speaking. I knew I didn't need to be alarmed at the figure. I simply knew I was safe.

'My name is John,' he introduced himself, 'I am Vincent's Grandfather.' The old man looked deep into my eyes. 'I have been over here a short time, but I need to tell the family that the electrics in the house are all wrong. They could cause a fire if they don't deal with them quickly.' He paused as a young lady joined him with the most beautiful flawless skin I have ever seen. She was gentle and caring toward the old man. Her fair hair tumbled down her shoulders and over the low neckline of her full gown of scintillating pastel colours. She radiated a feeling of love, so relaxing, so calming. Drawing the elderly man toward her, she smiled and gently showed him the way back to their world of sunshine. I watched as the two of them strolled toward the rose arch, then John escaped her gentle hold and quickly returned to me.

'Tell them to check the electrics in the house, before it goes up,' he urged. The beautiful lady caught up with him again and this time he returned with her into the heavenly garden. He wasn't angry or uncomfortable, in fact quite the opposite, happy to stroll arm in arm with this beautiful maiden. The light slowly faded into the reality of the night. Climbing the stairs two at a time, making as much noise as possible was Vince.

'Are you all right?' he queried, puffing and panting. A deep sigh from me was all I was able to answer. I could have cried buckets with relief. Instead I asked Vince if he had had a grandfather named 'John'. His face was a picture.

'Yes,' he answered slowly, 'But he died a few years ago. He was a funny old guy. He'd get up in the early hours to check the electrics all over the house. Light sockets, switches, anything he decided needed checking.' I stopped in my tracks and turned to face Vince.

'He was here tonight,' I told him. 'He told me to make sure you checked all the electrics in this house, he seemed convinced it would caused a house fire.' Though plainly he doubted me, Vince accepted the urgency in my voice and investigated the wiring downstairs in the box.

'I can't see anything,' he said, 'But tomorrow we'll call in an electrician. He can get this sorted out once and for all.' His tired voice showed the wear of the day. I was relieved when he said that no one would be staying at the house that night. I told the family that everything was now settled and peaceful again, promising them they would never hear from that particular spirit again. I said goodnight, wondering if it had all been a dream or a nightmare. But no, I knew it was real. The drive back to my own home couldn't pass fast enough for me, I just wanted a bath and to be with my family, safe.

All night I thought of nothing else. When Keith came home a little later on, he asked how the evening went.

'Fine,' I answered sleepily. I don't think I could ever fully tell him what had happened in that house that night, it was straight out of a horror film, but like all good stories this one had a happy ending.

The following day, Vince and Lisa told me that the priest had arrived that morning.

'What wonderful perfume has filled the air!' he declared. 'This house is clear of any problems.' As the family walked around the house, each room was filled with the perfume of the most beautiful English roses, which lasted for days on end.

'Oh, and by the way,' chorused Vince and Lisa, 'We called in an electrician, and oddly enough he found that some of the wiring had become loose, and said it could have caused a house fire at any time.' I spun around looking Vince straight in the face. 'Your grandfather was right, the house could have gone up in smoke. Thank God he was there.' Personally, I was relieved Sixpence was there too, with her friends. I don't know what I would have done without her and them.

Since it all happened I have been asked what caused the rest of the trouble. I could give many answers, and I don't think one of them would completely suffice. Things happen without much encouragement in many different circumstances, not one being the same as any other. All I know is, trouble came calling when that family's lives were unwittingly in danger. Maybe that was all that was needed to cause the lower levels to provide the most frightening array of terror imaginable, to that young family and me. I believe a potential poltergeist and haunting was in evidence in that house.

Since then, Lisa has had the baby she was expecting, safe and sound. I did not know she was pregnant but that must have added even greater terror to the night's events for both parents. Lisa and Vince have now left that house which was only rented and bought one of their own. I have heard nothing since, so I must assume everything is all right.

I enjoyed the remainder of the Christmas festivities after everything calmed down, that is until the phone rang again. Could I possibly go and visit a family whose television kept going on, even when it wasn't plugged in? As soon as I arrived at the house, I discovered a tremendous amount of energy. The source quickly became obvious. There was a young girl living there who was going through puberty creating all this energy. She was like an aerial swinging round out of control, and had been grabbed by a passing spirit. All this base energy needed an outlet. If she became involved in sports or the creative arts, peace would be restored. Often children like this become healers or mediums.

The chances of coming across a disruptive spirit are not as common as one might think. But after the Orthodox church had called me in a few times to do some work for them, word seemed to get around that I could cope with such spirits. Since then, I seem to have had more than my fair share. So I was not surprised when a gentleman from somewhere in England phoned to say that he'd had saucepans thrown at him by 'something' and he was very frightened.

'Can you come straight away? I'll pay for your travel,' he urged. 'Just come. No, not tomorrow. I need you now, before it throws anything else at me. I can't handle this. I don't believe in this kind of thing, so why should it pick on me? Catch the next train.' And he rang off. Fate seemed to be on my side for once. I managed to catch the first train to England and a taxi seemed to be waiting for me outside the station at the other end.

Ten minutes later I was staring up at the gentleman's home, as always checking the front of the property first. But the man who'd phoned me couldn't wait for that. He dashed out of the house and grabbed my arm hard, making me jump in shock. Looking round quickly to see if anyone was watching, he seemed relieved to realise the street was empty.

'Come in here,' he begged, leading me into one of the downstairs rooms. 'This is where the trouble started.' He looked so uptight.

'Can I walk around freely?' I asked gently. 'I need to feel the energies which are causing the problem.' Much to my surprise and discomfit, he pushed me into the next room, then upstairs. I found nothing in the other rooms, just a modicum of energy in the living room.

'There's nothing anywhere, except a small bit of energy in this room,' I explained to him, 'Sit down and tell me exactly what happened.' He wiped his brow with a large blue handkerchief and sitting down, nodded to himself as if coming to a decision.

'A few months ago a very dear friend of mine passed suddenly. He believed fervently in all these sorts of things,' he said, waving his hand in my direction. 'I was just telling my wife that it was all very silly, and that everyone knows that we are buried six foot down and that's that, when out of the blue a saucepan that my wife keeps plants in just took off. It flew over my head and back again with such force that I had to duck under a table to escape.' He stopped as if daring me to question his story. 'What on earth could it be?'

The spirit voice resounded in my ear before I could answer him.
'That will teach him a lesson,' said the angry voice in my ear. I was just as annoyed with my unseen visitor.

'You are wrong, my friend,' I advised. 'You should never behave like that.'
'Why not? He said I was as dead as a dodo and as you can tell, I'm not.'

'No one should be hurt by another's anger like that,' I retorted. 'What's more, you're abusing a power which could benefit others. You're wasting it on retaliation.'

Suddenly the spirit realised that I could hear what he was saying.
'I'm sorry,' he mumbled quietly. 'It won't happen again. That is, unless he starts again with his rubbish about the afterlife.' The gentleman who'd phoned me shook his head nervously as I told him the conversation.

'I still don't really believe you were talking to him. How do I know you aren't just making it all up?'

I asked the question of the spirit who chuckled.
'I'll show him. Tell him he needs to go and buy a new saucepan. He burnt one this morning. I was watching.'

When I relayed this message, the man who'd phoned me turned white and grasped the edge of the table in front of him.

'How on earth did he know that?

'There's only one way,' I smiled. 'He must have been here as he says he was.' He sat there, mulling this over, then asked if his friend from the spirit worlds had gone.

'Yes,' I replied.

'Good, I didn't like him much when he was here, I like him even less now.' He smiled a sickly smile at me, then jumped as the window suddenly rattled behind him. I smiled.

'Only a passing car,' I reassured him, getting up to leave. As we reached the door, he pushed something in my hand.

'Open it outside,' he muttered, closing the door with a thud. I looked at what he had put in my hand. A five-pound note - presumably my fare home - wrapped around a biscuit. He hadn't even offered me a cup of tea!

A young, terrified Nikita practically screamed down the phone line to me. Once I could understand her, I learnt that her mother was still experiencing terrible ugly and abusive treatment from Nikita's stepfather who had died two years ago. The poor girl sobbed as she told me what had happened. Mum had fallen into the trap of an abusive relationship which had lasted several years. Those of the   family who were old enough had all fled their home in fear of his torrents of abuse, unwillingly leaving Mum and the younger children to his explosive temper. Bruised and battered, the mother used all her strength many times to protect her remaining children from her abusive partner.

In what turned out to be his last heavy drinking bout, Nikita's stepfather fell from one public house to another on the council estate where they lived. So drunk he could barely stand, he staggered home, only to collapse on the pavement and choke to death on his own vomit. The reunited family enjoyed two peaceful years, until Mother fell in love with a lovely gentleman. Soon things began to happen. Coldness and an indescribable stench filled the house. Flowers were pulled from vases and thrown into the air. Doors slammed, curtains were pulled into disarray. Birthday presents from her now-departed mother were thrown at her. Mum began to think she was going mad.

Matters had come to a head that night when Mum was physically hit out of her chair and onto the floor. Just before Nikita had phoned me, Mum wrapped herself in a Welsh shawl for warmth, and ran out onto the street, begging Nikita to find someone, anyone, who could put an end to this abuse which she now realised had to be coming from her dead husband. All the neighbours were out on the street as well, attracted by the noise and wondering just what was going on. While friends comforted her mother, Nikita frantically phoned mediums, healers, anyone whose number she could find but no one would venture forward. However, they all volunteered one name, mine! Thanks a bunch!

I quickly arrived at the house and as usual scanned the outside, searching for an imbalance, which would tell me where the culprit was. Downstairs, curtains waved to and fro. Pathetic, I thought, knowing the spirit could read my mind. If that was meant to frighten me, you're wrong.

'I'll need your mum to be close at hand while I work.' I explained to Nikita.

'No chance,' Nikita refused vehemently.
'I'm sorry but Mum's the target of the abuse and therefore the one who will attract her husband's spirit. Wherever your mother goes, he'll go too. It's no use her going next door in the hope that he'll stay in your house. He'll just go next door with her.' Partly reassured, Nikita reluctantly agreed.

'No one's going to hurt you or your Mum anymore,' I promised, boiling over with fury at such behaviour in anyone, let alone a spirit. The living room curtains were still waving so I took it he was still in there.

'We'll have to go into the house now.' I explained. 'Try not to feel afraid, fear just gives him something to feed on and makes him strong.' We all took deep breaths and clutching one another's hands bonebreakingly tight, went into the house. Gently, a spirit I recognised as little Sixpence edged over to my side.

'Leave this to us,' she purred. 'But tell everyone what we are doing.'
'No problem,' I replied.

The air was thick with hatred and fear. Cold shivers ran up and down my spine -Sixpence, letting me know she was close by. I closed the door behind the last person, only to have it thrown open again with terrific force. A ghostly man, tall and strong, rushed past everyone, heading for Mum, closely followed by two larger spirit men who grabbed his arms with such force that he screamed loudly. His eyes opened widely, eyebrows arched, as he flung his head from side to side, trying to throw off his captors. As he was forced to about turn and frog-marched out towards the cold night air, the prisoner fought with all his might against his warders. My heart lurched as he grabbed the door handle. The jolt loosened his captors' hold and he swung himself around and away from his guards, back into the living room.

But the spirit realms had another trick up their sleeve. Four of the largest spirit dogs I have ever seen growled and snarled at his heels as he raced across the room. Yelping as they nipped his heels, he tripped over the chairs, then jumped over the table and ran back through the front door and away from his warders and the house as fast as he could. Everyone was delighted when I described what had happened. Mother and daughter fell into each other's arms, weeping with relief and thanking me over and over.

'Has he really gone, Frances?' they asked me, their tear-soaked faces breaking into smiles. Mum cupped her hands to her face as she felt the tears of relief wash away years of torment. She smiled uncertainly as she dried her face with a large handkerchief.

'I'm sorry for being so silly. You must think me a right fool.'
'No need, it's simply a cleansing and healing,' I offered quietly. A calmness engulfed the room as Mum settled in her chair.

'He has gone now, hasn't he, love?' she asked again anxiously. I nodded in agreement, but something was still puzzling me.

'It's just those dogs,' I said. 'They were so huge. I've never seen anything like them in any of the work the spirit team has done before.' Mum chuckled.

'Oh, that's easy. My old man was petrified of dogs, wouldn't go two streets near them. He got his just rewards tonight, didn't he, love?' With Mum's peace of mind restored and confidant that he would not return, I left the house, knowing the four dogs were still prowling round, loyally staying with Mum. But I knew there was no real need, he would not be back. Holding my arm tightly, Nikita walked down the driveway of the house with me after I'd said my farewell to Mum.

'Is this likely to happen again?' she asked, still obviously concerned. 'It would finish my mother if she had to endure that horror over again, Fran.' I turned to face her, looking straight into her swollen red eyes.

'Never again will you or your family be subjected to such terror. I promise you.' Nikita hugged me tightly.

'You are special, you know, Fran.' She smiled warmly.
'No, love, just a medium with pretty special friends in my corner.'
Last I heard he had given himself up to those who could guide him to a place

where he will learn to treat others with respect. He will stay there for quite a while. No one breaks spirit laws and gets away with it. It never fails to amaze me how the spirit realms find the exact solution for every problem they face. I had no idea that, that beast of a spirit would have any fears whatsoever, let alone that it would be dogs. I saw some of the biggest ugliest mutts in Christendom that day and wasn't I glad they were there. The spirit realms had the situation sussed straightaway. Only one word for them, brilliant.

I'm often asked if this kind of thing happens often. Of course some nasty characters occasionally slip through the spiritual net. Part of a medium's job is to assist in their capture. But I'm glad to say it's a bit like buses, nothing then a couple come along at once.

Fig.1 Twenty-four hours after the raging flames were extinguished and after a simple spirit reading with the late mother of an African gentleman (his domineering mother he claimed was a Voodoo Princess) the ghostly fire rages on. Several photos were taken along with this one but it remains the only one - all others have vanished.

Chapter Nine

Lost Souls

There are very special people whose sole function and spiritual path in this world is to encourage the rescue of souls which are lost and searching for help. Equally, there are those in the spirit worlds who work to aid such rescues. We work as a team. It is very challenging and rewarding work and a very special gift. It should certainly not be tried out by anyone who is not experienced in at least one area of mediumship. After all, we would not send anyone into a drugstore to freely choose their own medication. That is the job of the experienced pharmacist on the premises - in control, on their side of the counter, understanding and knowing what could damage you, even fatally, and of course what can help bring relief to many sicknesses. Although we do prefer the nicer side of this work, the rewards are wonderful whatever we do.

Christmas trimmings glittered through the smoke-filled room of the local social club. The Burma Star Association's Christmas party was in full swing. Volunteers from the audience of old comrades got up and sang or recited a poem, bringing laughter and smiles from everyone. This was my first visit to the Association's Christmas party. My mind returned time and time again to the dreadful times so many of them had endured during the wars. Many men and women there had fought in some of the greatest campaigns of the Second World War. Some, I knew, had been sent on very special missions, missions which still remained very hush, hush. So many had been prisoners of war. One sitting next to me showed me his hands, shaking with age, flecked with time, abuse and wear. He explained that the ghostly white mottled pigment of his skin was the result of damage inflicted in a camp in Burma. He was constantly having tumours removed from his stomach, the result of damage caused by the camp guards brutally beating him with a rifle butt each morning. During the course of the evening, we discovered that the ages of three gentlemen present added up to two hundred and sixty years.

The live entertainment ended for a short time and they started playing records of a bygone age. Many of the older gentlemen rose from their seats and slowly took their chosen companions onto the dance floor for the dance they humorously called the 'Zimmer waltz'.

I sang along to the well-known war tunes with the rest of the crowd. By the time we reached the end of the songs, we were all belting out the words, with the same fervour that must have accompanied them during the long ago days of war. I gradually became aware that misty forms, drawn by the singing and the memories, had gathered around the tables and chairs. Airmen, sailors and soldiers long gone in battle added their voices to those around me. It became an evening of rare comradeship for earth and spirit people alike.

The evening reminded me of an experience I'd had of helping a soldier of misfortune, one who died a long time ago in the horrors of the long past. I was at home with a small group who met once a week in a room shut away from the rest of the house. The room was nothing glamorous, just a few chairs forming a circle. The heavy curtains were drawn so that natural light could not peek through and a soothing audiotape played on my old and battered tape recorder. Everyone in the group enjoyed coming to help the spirit world as we never experienced the same thing two weeks running. The circle guides chose each evening's format. Sometimes we helped each other by working with the spirit guides as healer and patient, other times we experimented with something new. We all respected one another's work, taking pride in maintaining the highest standards in our communications with the spirit world. We always worked for no more than an hour and a half. That's quite long enough at any one sitting, it's very easy to get dehydrated and exhausted during this sort of session so I always made sure there was plenty of water for energy.

This particular evening was following our usual pattern. Music gently soothed away the day's rush, a prayer of love and protection was dedicated, someone turned down the lamp so that we would be able to see anything or anyone approaching our circle of love. In the warm and welcoming atmosphere we relaxed, hardly able to keep our eyes open. Our breathing became one. Such a relaxed state induces complete calm, with everybody still aware of any movement or sound independent of the group.

The already dimly lit room began to grow darker and colder by the second. Gentle breezes blew over our faces, and the faint smell of sulphur from gunfire engulfed the room. Quietly, we were able to see the outline of a person and heard what sounded like a rustle of paper in the corner of the room. We could all see and feel the presence of a soul watching us. Standing about five foot five tall, he wore a great coat. We could faintly see a hat or helmet, but it was not clear enough to see what shape it was or what badges adorned it. There also appeared to be straps of some kind binding his boots. This man had visited our group several times before, but we had never managed to keep him long enough to discover who he was or what he wanted. He always took a great deal of notice of what we as a group were doing though he moved out of sight at every opportunity before vanishing at the end of the evening. Tonight as usual he seemed too frightened to move toward us.

At this point helpers from the unseen world of light joined us. Rainbows of coloured lights encircled us like a protective band of heavenly auras. Suddenly the rainbow lights dimmed as if to allow the soldier to progress toward us, though he still took each step very gingerly. He slowly moved in and out of the shadows, seemingly not realising we could see him. Gradually he allowed himself to be seen, though not completely at first. His head moved slowly on his short shadowy frame as he tried to take in his surroundings. Obviously nervous, he chose to stand back out of the light, keeping in the shadows just outside our circle, watching.

Normally we ignored him until he made the first move. However, this evening, I had become decidedly drowsy, which everyone in our circle knew to be the sign of work. Each member of the group could see his forlorn outline and feel the coldness belonging to those in the spirit body. An air of weariness and sadness surrounded him. I hoped he would allow me to converse on his behalf to the others. I asked him mentally why he sought us out.

'Bill, just Bill. Call me that, it'll do,' said the forlorn soldier. I related what he was telling me to the rest of the group. 'I've been wandering for a long time. Something happened while we were in France, fighting in the war. The lights of the guns still went on but the guns were quiet. I can't work it out. No one could hear me. I tried to get their attention, as I could see a great light on the hill yonder. Hoards of men seemed to be going into this light, deserters, I suppose they were.' I could hear the tears in his voice. He little knew the lights of the final journey to the next life are brightly lit for all those whose lives have come to an end.

Suddenly I felt an overwhelming force of fear around this poor soul as he related the carnage he last recalled from so many years before. Suddenly to my delight, Sixpence appeared to me and explained that this tired and confused old soldier refused to allow anyone to help him. It seemed the lights of the spirit worlds had reminded him all too forcibly of the last moments of his life. As guns and lights lit up the night sky, screams from those around him and the smell of death prevented his transition to a place of peace. Although he couldn't hear the sounds, he could see the lights and, confused and refusing to be helped, he believed the great guns were still roaring.

Sixpence came up with a marvellous plan. If I could gain Bill's confidence, she would arrange for his family, who were already in the spirit world, to meet him in a nearby garden which was barely lit, in the hope that this would not upset this confused man.

Bill agreed to let me help him, on the understanding that if he should feel he was not ready, he could return to me until he felt the time was right. I watched as cautiously he walked with Sixpence. I'd expected him to look back but he didn't falter once as he followed Sixpence up to the dim garden. For the first time he began to accept that with help he could be released from his binds of fear. The entire group began to feel excited as Bill clung tightly to Sixpence's hand and made no moves to run away.

Sixpence was true to her word. The area was dimly lit, with park benches here and there alongside a meandering pathway. Tall posts, like Victorian gas lamps, dotted the park. It was so peaceful. A feeling of security blended with the lush green bushes and pale coloured flowers. There were no gates to keep people out, no railings surrounding the tall trees, no shadows dominating the area. From the other direction a lady could be heard calling. She reached out to Bill with open arms, calling out his name, and laughing and crying at the same time. Her long dress swept the path's surface, her small hands pressed down a crossover pinafore. As she drew closer to Bill, she cupped her hands together in pleasure. Bill looked at the lady. None of us knew who she was but Bill obviously did. His shoulders slumped down, then began to jerk up and down, as the experience became too much for him. He began to sob, he was almost home. Through tear-filled eyes, I watched an old soldier home from the battlefield greeted by his loved one. Tears ran down the lady's face as he held her long and hard. Just two people reunited again, forever. No more death, no more war, no more separations. Just a lifetime together, living in harmony, meeting old friends and comrades. It was the beginning of a healing. A simple wave of his hand and he strolled arm in arm with his special lady by his side, up the winding pathway out of sight.

Once Bill had left the circle, we all felt such relief and a rush of emotion as tears welled up in our throats and fits of coughing seemed to overtake other members of the group. Suddenly nearby the tip of an unlit candle jumped into flame burning brightly and then promptly extinguishing itself. I think we all jumped out of our skins. Of course it was the spirit realms letting us know that it was all right for Bill to enter the light of the world of the spirits without fear or apprehension. The room grew warm and friendly, there was an overwhelming air of happiness and contentment. Still we sat in subdued light, strange how it seemed so much lighter in that room that night. A comforting sort of glow melted into the atmosphere. I think we all wanted to be with someone we loved that night, to share the experience of two people who had found each other at last.

We spoke for an age afterwards. Who would have thought that someone so long ago could still be suffering from a terrible war long over? He must have wandered for years, too afraid to simply 'go over' for fear of those lights. What fear must have filled those young men on the battle grounds of long ago, that they were unable to follow the natural urge to complete life itself and move on. How many more are still suffering the same plight, we asked ourselves. So often Sixpence and John Redmond have told me of those who, because of their sudden Transition, feel so solid in their bodies that they often become confused when told they have made the change from this life. So convinced are they that they are still alive that they often argue the point, and why not? If you see that you have all your bits and pieces, wouldn't you argue too?

I'd just come out of the shower one morning when a terrific thundering on my front door reverberated throughout the house. I quickly wrapped myself in a dressing gown and ran to the door, alarmed by the racket and wondering what the problem could possibly be.

A slightly built woman was hammering on it, screaming for all she was worth, beside herself with fear.

'Come on,' she screamed, grabbing hold of the sleeve of my dressing gown. 'You are the medium, aren't you?'

'Yes, I am, but calm down. I can't do anything until you tell me what the problem is.' Gently I persuaded her into the living room where she collapsed onto the sofa. As I sat down beside her, she grabbed my arm again.

'You've got to help me, you've just got to.'

'Of course I will,' I promised. 'You live in that flat over the shop on the corner, don't you?' She nodded.

'That's the problem. You've got to come back there with me now. I can't go back there on my own, I just can't.' She crouched into the back of the sofa and stared around in terror.

'It's all right, love. You're safe here. Whatever frightened you at home wouldn't dare follow you here, you have my word on that. Now then, I don't even know your name.' She took a deep breath and gave me a watery smile.

'It does feel safe here, thank goodness. You must think me daft. My name's Karen, by the way. We've only lived in the flat for a couple of months but we were really beginning to settle down. People are so friendly round here and that matters to us.

My husband works away a lot, see, and he worries about me on my own. Don't know what he'll say when he finds out what happened this morning. We'll have to move again, can't stay here no more.' I moved into the kitchen to make a cup of tea. 'We don't have time for tea, you gotta come back to the flat with me now. It might go before we get there, then I'll never know when it's coming back again.'

'Don't you think you'd better explain just what did visit you this morning? And don't worry, we've time for tea. I'll soon sort it out, whatever it is and wherever it's gone.' Over tea, Karen explained the morning's events.

'Mr Jenkins, him who owned the shop and the flat, you know he died last week?' I nodded, remembering the cantankerous old man who'd run the corner shop. 'Me and Gary never met him, he'd been in hospital ever since we moved in. His son deals with the rent. Well, things were fine in the flat until three days ago, the day they buried Mr Jenkins. Since then, all sorts of things have been happening. Funny knocks and doors slamming, cold draughts round our feet.

We thought the flat just needed some more insulation, Gary was going to talk to Mr Jenkins's son when he got back this weekend. He's a long distance lorry driver, see, works all over Europe.' I filled her mug with fresh tea.

'So what happened this morning? Not just some more draughts, I take it?' She shook her head, terror returning to her face.

'I just knew there was somebody in the flat. I was washing up after breakfast and I turned round and there was this figure sort of standing behind me. I screamed but it just seemed to pick me up and carried me into the hall and dropped me on the floor.' She took a large gulp of tea. Wondering if perhaps her imagination had been playing tricks on her in an empty flat, I mentally asked the spirit realms to confirm her story. They swiftly told me everything she'd told me had happened. Suddenly I was filled with fury.

'You wait there while I get dressed,' I told Karen. 'Just who does he think he is, bullying you like that? I'll soon sort him out.' As I dressed hastily, my stomach was turning somersaults and my hands shook, but I knew I couldn't allow any spirit to abuse people like that.

Karen and I dashed to her flat, the door of which was at the side of the empty shop. Carefully, I scanned the outside of the property, to assess the feel of the place, then slowly opened the front door leading upstairs to the offending living room and bedroom. I could feel cold spots all around the flat but one room in particular was intensely dense and cold. Immediately, I was aware of a spirit. He was thickly built with a belligerent air about him.

'Who the hell are you?' he demanded. 'Just how many more of you are there? Get out of my flat and take her with you. Thought I'd got rid of her once already.' I looked past him and could see another spirit, a female one this time.

'Hello, my name's Ruth, I'm Karen's grandmother. I've been in the spirit world for quite a few years now and have always kept a close eye on Karen. I've been trying to protect her from this man but I just can't seem to get through to him.' The male spirit ignored our conversation, shambling round the room and eying up Karen.

'You leave her alone,' I warned him. 'Now you just tell me why you're giving her such a hard time.'

'This whole building's mine,' he protested, clearing his throat. 'I paid for it and I don't want any old Tom, Dick or Harry living here, so she can get out before I throw her out again. They've all got a bloody cheek.' This told me all I needed to know. He was obviously lost and unaware of his death. When this happens, a spirit remains earthbound and often causes havoc until it can be helped over into the spirit realms. I had to act quickly. The last thing I wanted was for things to get out of hand. I tried to calm the situation by sending him compassionate thoughts. As I concentrated, his anger subsided and calm filled the room. My next move was vitally important. He had to remain convinced I was there to help him. I needed his confidence and the help of the spirit world to bring about some measure of peace. At least by hearing him out, I could keep the atmosphere more relaxed, then hopefully find a solution for everybody. I knew I could count on Ruth to help by urging his loved ones to come close to him. I hoped it would work. Slowly, my voice steadied.

'Have you felt a change in yourself?' He thought about the question for so long I feared he was going to ignore me.

'Might have.'

'Have any of your relatives behaved oddly when you spoke to them?'

'Yes. How do you know that?' I hoped my next question would help him realise that he had exchanged his physical body for a spiritual one. As carefully as I could, so as not to shock him too much, I asked the crucial question.

'Can you recall a family gathering where everyone seemed to be in tears? Can you remember them ignoring all your efforts to comfort them?' I could see in his face the moment the truth dawned.

'I'm a goner, am I?' he asked. I nodded solemnly.

'If you look around you, you can see your loved ones who have already gone on. They've tried to reach you, but you made it too difficult.' As we'd been talking, the room had gradually filled up with his spirit family, and I could clearly hear sighs and welcome sounds coupled with tears of relief. Now that he understood the situation, I knew Mr Jenkins would allow Karen to live in the flat in peace. He also agreed not to disturb whatever business opened up downstairs. Karen was happy, Ruth was happy as she had played a big part in helping me to encourage the man to find his peace of mind. And Mr Jenkins was happy now he knew that people only seemed to be ignoring him because they couldn't see him. He was indeed content to find that loved ones he had not seen for many years were welcoming him into their arms. I was happy because I could go home and eat my lunch, I'd missed breakfast. God's in his heaven, all's well with the world.

I never heard any more from Karen, so everything must be OK. The shop has since been filled with stock and business has not been interrupted by any ex-landlord.

You may wonder why I was so careful not to cause shock to that spirit gentleman. Well, imagine, if you can, what you would feel if someone blurted out that you were dead. The shock in a soul may cause them unlimited problems and it takes no longer to explain the transition gently and in a comforting way.

Chapter Ten

Graveside manner

Even though I hadn't seen my uncle for more than twenty years, I still became very worried when I heard he had been admitted to hospital with dreadful head pains. I had such fond memories of him and regretted that I hadn't managed to visit him more often but holding down a full-time job and taking care of the family left me with little spare time. I resolved to make an effort to visit him when he recovered but in the meantime I just had to wait for news of him, as the rest of the family had to do.

Some days later, at work, I developed an unexpected migraine. I tried hard to pass it off but it continued to plague me. I felt dreadful. I just simply could not think clearly and was more of a hindrance than a help to my colleagues so was ushered off home to rest. I can recall very little of that after-noon. I tried to rest in complete darkness, unable to think or see properly. The headache finally left me at about six the same evening.

Some time later, a relative mentioned how much my uncle stated how he had enjoyed his half hour's chat with me before his wife appeared at visiting time. No one could have been more surprised than I at this information. I probed to find out when I had supposedly visited the hospital. To my amazement, I discovered it coincided with that migraine.

Shortly afterwards he passed away. I felt disappointed that I had failed to see him in time and so I made the effort some time later to visit his grave. I didn't want to upset anyone by asking where I could find his grave, so I decided to go along to the cemetery and hope to come across it for myself. Unfortunately there were several cemeteries close together and I had no way of knowing which one my uncle was in. I looked around at the thousands of neatly laid-out graves in the first cemetery. It would be like looking for a needle in a haystack but I was determined that if it took all day, I was going to find my uncle's resting-place.

I strolled along, glancing up and down at each headstone in the hope of finding one with his name on it. A few yards away, I spotted a bench, just the thing for tired legs. The sun shone warmly that day. Occasionally a breeze blew up, rustling the leaves on the old trees and disturbing the fresh flowers on the grave-stones, but at least it cooled my face as well.

When I reached the little bench, I sat down thankfully and glanced around the huge cemetery. I still had a very large amount of graves to look at. As I swept my hair from my hot face yet again, the annoying wind stopped abruptly. A feeling of complete silence and peace filtered everywhere. Not one sound did I hear. Cars racing past outside faded away. Birds normally full of song were silent.

I dug deep into my handbag for the can of lukewarm drink I had bought earlier. A movement a few feet away caught my eye and I looked up eagerly, hoping it was someone I could ask about my uncle's grave. Two gentlemen wearing dark modern-day suits stepped out from behind a tree. They were obviously spirit forms, though I felt quite surprised that they looked so solid. As they strolled towards me, the larger of the two seemed to be having an intense conversation with his smaller companion, who seemed to be nodding quite often. This was just the opportunity I was looking for. Who better than the spirit realms to answer a simple question? They were sure to know where my uncle lay to rest, I thought.

'Excuse me,' I asked, rising from the bench to approach them. 'I wonder if you could help me. I am looking for my uncle's grave and hoped you may have seen it on your way here. I realise you are spirits and hope you may be of some he...' The words were hardly out of my mouth when the wind blew up fiercely again. The larger of the two gentlemen grew very angry that I could see and talk to them.

'I've heard of people like you,' he thundered loudly. 'Get out of this place. We don't want the likes of you in here. Out, get out!!!'

I became very nervous, not knowing what this person would do next. I breathed in deeply, feeling my temper rise in response to his aggression. The wind grew stronger and noisier. The strap of my handbag broke under the pressure and flew away from me. The wind gusted around my large frame with such power and strength that I was spun round several times, then driven back towards the main gates of the cemetery. I don't take kindly to being forced to do something I don't want to do, so I forced my way back into the cemetery, brushing away the leaves and dry grass which clung to my dress.

As I forced my way back towards them, the larger abusive individual stormed off in obvious disgust. The smaller mousy-looking spirit stepped towards me hesitantly, looking over his shoulder at his companion.

'I'm sorry for that,' he explained. 'He has the old beliefs.' I felt rather sorry for him but was keen to see how he'd explain away his companion's total abuse of spirit power. 'I am afraid he doesn't take kindly to people like you. You worry him. He thinks you're here to create damage. You see, he thinks he's still alive, he's understandably confused by everything that's happened. I've been given the task of telling him of his demise but he refuses to believe me.' I listened intently as this little person tried to make me understand. 'I have a duty to those who have passed on. I help them understand their fate. 'They' call us the caretakers.' His eyes rolled upwards, as if some angel were hovering above him. 'We are self-appointed to bring people such as my friend to some sort of acceptance of their plight.' As he turned and followed his companion, one last word filtered back to me. 'Sorry.'

So was I. People like me can and do speak to those we call the departed but this does not make me a devil. The smaller man most certainly understood that people like me can communicate, as we did when the other chap turned his back on me. Although he was very nervous, he was able to speak to me and I could answer him. Maybe there is a need for these caretakers as they call themselves. I had never heard of this particular form of care before that day, and have not experienced it again, thank goodness.

Still shaken by the encounter, I crossed the road and entered another cemetery, having no idea where I was going. Oddly, I found my uncle's grave straightaway. It seemed as if a loving hand guided me right up to it. Naturally, I would like to think it was my uncle or perhaps another soul who'd seen what had just happened. I did not attempt to find out which. The fact that I found the grave was enough for one day. In the second cemetery I did not come into contact with a 'caretaker' and the wind did not rise up at all. It was just how you would expect a garden of rest to be - peaceful. I learnt a lesson that day. Never stop a spirit in the cemetery and ask the way to a loved one's grave. They put the wind up you.

Chapter Eleven

Bad experience

You're relaxing on a lovely holiday with your husband and basking in the sun at the hotel's pool. Suddenly a tremendous surge of pain shoots through your whole body. After the pain has ceased, all you're aware of is the sheer horror of seeing yourself lying on the ground. People are rushing around wildly, shouting, waving their arms about. Your husband crouches tearfully over what seems to be your still body, while you look on in utter shock at all the fuss. Questions race through your mind. Why are people running around? Why am I lying on the ground and how is it I can see myself lying there? You call to your husband but he's too wrapped up in cradling your body to take any notice. So you start shouting but that doesn't seem to work either. Taking a deep breath, you scream his name but still no response. This is little short of a nightmare. Just what is happening? The emergency services carry your body out of the glare and you know you must follow them. As the ambulance rushes away from the hotel, you push people aside as you try to keep up with it. You don't realise these people are calling your name and trying to help you. Your eyes are firmly fixed on the ambulance and nothing is going to stop you following it. Finally you reach the hospital. You realise several men dressed as paramedics are following you but something tells you they aren't there to help you. No genuine paramedic could look so threatening. As you run away from them, they follow. No matter how fast you run, they seem to have no trouble keeping up with you. Sweating, tired and confused, you try to find a room to hide in but each time you are almost caught. You run out of the hospital by the nearest door and race down a side alley and into the town itself. You must escape from these men but you have no idea where you are or which way is safe. Leaning against a wall to catch your breath, you start to accept that a tremendous change has happened in your life. The specialist had warned you that you needed to take better care of your heart but you now realise the warning came too late. Tears fill your eyes as you accept the fact that you must have died back at the swimming pool. The most sensible thing to do now is to get back home where you'll be safe from these horrible men.

Back in your hotel room, you reach out your hand towards your husband. You have such a need to comfort him as he sits on the bed, crying out in his grief for you. But although you sit next to him on the bed, he doesn't know you are there. He can't see or hear you. Tears of grief and frustration pour down your face too. If only he could realise you were right there with him.

Bright lights stream around the room, causing you to shield your eyes. Strange how they don't seem to affect your husband. He even gets up to light the lamps beside the bed. You wonder just why he seems to need extra light but watch as he packs his cases and yours. He breaks down in renewed tears as he carefully folds that new dress of yours which you were saving for dinner on the last night of the holiday, the dress that was going to make you look so fantastic, just for him. Now you're just longing for a cup of tea and an explanation of the day's events.

Suddenly you hear voices, the voices of the paramedics rushing down the corridor towards your room. You turn to your husband in terror but he is still packing and seems not to hear the commotion outside. You realise that you alone can hear them and it's up to you to escape them again. Panic fills you as you realise that the only way out of the room is blocked by the men but then you remember that you'd been able to walk through walls during your earlier escape. Swallowing hard, you pray that you will be able to do it again. If you do not hurry, your husband will have left the hotel without you, leaving you to the mercy of those men. Slipping carefully through the hotel you are free, away from the grasp of those three paramedics.

All the way home you try to talk to your husband. It's a waste of time, he can't hear you. You cry bitterly and angrily scream your husband's name into his face. It achieves nothing! The house you bought together stands dark. Tired but relieved, you drag yourself out of the car and into the home you shared as man and wife. The telephone rings, your grownup children ask if they can join their father in his grief. Right now all you need is sleep.

But you hear heavy footsteps somewhere close at hand. You begin to shake but you know crying won't help. The only thing you can do is to hide away once more from the aggressive army of men out to do you harm. Tucked away out of their sight for a moment, you use the time to think fast. Who can help you? Who is involved in this kind of thing, these living ghosts, as those hunting you down seem to be? You have so many questions and no answers. If you are dead, where is Heaven? The answers to your prayer comes in a flash. Your minister will know what to do. Gliding silently out of the house to avoid alerting the paramedics again, you race to your minister's home. The lights are still on in his study and somehow you are standing in front of his desk where he seems to be reading his Bible before retiring for the night. But despite your pleading and tears, he looks straight through you and putting out the lights, climbs the stairs to bed. You collapse sobbing at the bottom of the staircase. The whole world has gone mad. In the corner of your eye you spot a light, gentle, calming. You gasp in shock then realise in amazement that you were still breathing. Maybe you weren't dead after all? Perhaps this is only a nightmare and you'll wake up in a minute? Oh, this is becoming so confusing. If you are not dead, why did you see your own body taken into an ambulance and how could you walk through walls?

Determined to find out the truth, you make your way back home again, leaving the minister to his sleep. Just before you reach home, the noise of heavy footsteps behind you sparks the panic again. Where can you find a safe hiding place? If you are dead and this is heaven, you can keep it. Dodging behind the thick hedge bordering the road, you peer down at yourself to see a bedraggled body, grubby from earth's thick fog of ignorance. Your clothes stick to you in the heat of rushing around trying to avoid the 'men'. You still don't know who they are, and you don't want to know. All you want is to be left alone to think and recover. You need a plan. You need help. You need a miracle. Suddenly Patrick springs to mind. Wasn't he something to do with the spiritualist church, a healer or something? He has to help, there is no one else. You sink down realising there's nothing you can do until the morning. Patrick will be long in bed and you know you don't have the strength or the knowledge to wake him up.

Next morning as soon as the world begins to stir, you make your way quietly round to Patrick's studio at the bottom of his garden. You haven't slept much. The men didn't materialise again but you spent the whole night jumping in terror at the slightest sound. Patrick is an old friend, an artist, who built his studio at the end of his garden for peace and quiet. You peer through his window.

He's whistling quietly to himself. Wave at him, he's sure to see you.

'Patrick,' you call loudly, 'It's me.' He looks up briefly. A sharp intake of breath, tears again, only this time they are tears of joy. 'Patrick, you heard me.'

Again. You must do it again. This time, Patrick walks out of his studio, locking the door behind him. Running in front of him, you wave your arms in his face. He stops, stares at you, and returns to the studio. Your heart sinks. He didn't see you, he was thinking about his latest painting and realised he had forgotten something in his workshop. Yet you feel sure he saw you, or saw something. There was a chance, a slim chance, Again you rush around him. He shivers, then looking bewildered, he speaks in hushed tones.

'Hello, spirit,' he whispers quietly. Your eyes fill up. At long last someone knows you are there, but he does not see you and is unable to converse with you. You need to make a decision - you keep bothering Patrick, or keep running from those men. No contest really. You would keep visiting Patrick until he finds out who you are. You abandon trying to speak directly to him and concentrate on penetrating his mind instead. Patrick has returned to his studio to look for an important letter which you can see is buried under a mass of papers.

'Help me,' you call, putting all your energy into the cry. Patrick drops the books he's lifting in shock. He's heard you! He shakes his head in denial and carries on looking for the letter. You don't believe this, he obviously thinks he's hearing things. You'll just have to try again. This time there's no mistaking his response.

'Sarah? Is that you? If it is, help me find this letter, then I'll know I'm not hearing things.'

'There is a god after all,' you whisper to yourself. You take a deep breath and pray you have enough energy for him to hear you again. 'Over there in the drawer under the papers.' The thought wings through the shed. For one awful moment you think he hasn't heard you, then he swings round and makes straight for the desk. Waving the letter in the air, he turns back towards you.

'Thank you, Sarah. It really must be you. I can't tell you how dreadful it was to hear about your news. But what are you doing here? Is there a problem? Let me get hold of my daughter. Remember her? She's a medium. If anyone can help you, she can.'

Relief sweeps through you, help at last. But suddenly the heavy thud of boots are coming towards you again. Oh no! it can't be, not those creatures again. In despair, you realise they have found you again. You can't stay in Patrick's studio, you have to run, just run anywhere, somewhere dark and quiet, until they are gone. Why won't they give up? What do they need with you? You have nothing they could want. Even your life is not yours anymore.

It seems like days pass by, while you hide in cold spots, alone, no one to hold you, no one to tell you that you're missed. You catnap, waiting for someone to help you out of this horror film called death. Where is Patrick? Has he abandoned you like everyone else?

Suddenly, you are drawn into a rush of spiralling mists, lit by waves of colours, towards a brilliant circle of light. Your chest beats with fear. Closer and closer you are pulled into a house, trying to cling onto anything to prevent yourself from entering. It's still earth, you assess wildly. You are spun around until you land softly on your feet. There are people, sitting in a complete circle, chanting the Lord's Prayer over and over. In the centre, the light spins, like a fountain of coloured lights, sparkling around and around. You are caught up in the centre, jostled by the force of the energy. You feel warmth and a love never before felt. Confused but still aware of the dangers, you call out into the light. People you know, Patrick, he's there, and there's Patrick's daughter. She is asking you to draw forward so that she can help you. This is no time to argue. As you walk towards her, you see others behind the medium. They welcome you also but they don't look the same as the rest of the group. They are in body just like you. Feeling limp from your experiences you suddenly give in, sinking down to be caught by the medium who has also come out of her body.

'Are you dead too?' you ask, astonished. You can see her empty body slumped in the chair. She shakes her head and holds your hand firmly. You begin to feel hope and surrender the situation to the medium. You are going to be saved after all. You look round at the scene you are leaving. Everyone is in tears. Slowly, you and the medium rise up off the floor. Outside the circle of energy, lights dash round and round as the paramedics try to break the grip of the circle of friends but even though they are big men, they are weak against the power of the circle. At long last you are safe, amongst friends. The medium comforts you, telling you not to let go of her hand. You swear never to let go, ever. Squeezing her hand as hard as you can somehow makes you feel that much stronger, confident even.

The two of you begin to float upwards through what resembles a round and very wide brick-built chimney. It's night at the bottom where you started off, yet near the top, a beautiful summer's day greets you, blue skies and fluffy white clouds. Then astonishingly, familiar faces appear at the top of the chimney.

'Margaret,' you call out, then 'Albert.' The medium lets go of your hand, she is not allowed to enter the top of the chimney. But you don't mind now. In disbelief you are helped out of the passage of hope and into the arms of these wonderful people who have come to greet you after your horrific journey. When you are sufficiently rested, you will return to thank the people who ended your nightmare. Until then, you will rest.

Heaven looks pretty good right now.

This story is true. I knew the lady in spirit and was the medium who helped her find peace. The woman herself gave me the full account of her experiences. Purely by chance, one day, I asked a friend of hers who Margaret and Albert could possibly be, and learned they were her brother and sister. They had passed to the spirit world some eight years and five years before.

I put you in the part of the spirit so that you may understand her fears and how she handled her situation. Also it explains the importance of a rescue circle. The spirit in this story has since been back to thank me. Those who made her journey such hell have never been seen since. My personal view is that 'they' had come from the lower levels, where the Hitlers of this world end up. She had mistakenly wandered into 'their' world. It is rare that such a rescue is needed. In fact I have never had to deal with another mess as horrifying as the one I found her in that day.

Whatever she stumbled on made her the victim of a gang, but they were unable to break through the sacred circle of love and prayer my friends built with the aid of the spirit world. Silently the guides overpowered the ruthless thugs chasing a lone woman. With their help I was able to assist her into the Summerland, amongst those who had tried to reach out to her earlier on, without much success. They were the lights she'd spotted back at the hotel. Her fears had masked her rescue at that point. I have helped many into the spirit world, and again I must repeat myself, I swear this was the only one who slipped through the net of angels into sheer terror. Normally, someone will meet us. A loved one gone to the world of the spirit or a person chosen for their love of you will return to take us across the great divide.

Chapter Twelve
Before life

We were delighted when our eldest daughter Julie met and settled down with Mathew. They decided to start a family immediately but sadly Julie miscarried her first baby, which made us all grieve for her and Mathew. A child would have been the icing on the cake. When she told us she was pregnant again, we were naturally overjoyed, yet worried for her. Soon the weeks built into months. The longer she carried the baby, the more cautiously excited we became but problems began to show as Julie entered her testing third month. Over the following weeks, her difficulties became our main concern but, despite all the worries, I instinctively knew that she would be strong enough to endure her pregnancy.

But my worries still stopped me concentrating properly on my work so I turned to John Redmond, my spirit guide, for help. I decided to stay up later than usual one night, knowing that John would help me in my dilemma. Soon he moved to my side, then he took my spirit body into the spirit realms. We strolled together arm in arm up a path leading to a great hospital. Walking like this felt so familiar, as if we had enjoyed these walks before in another time.
The spirit sun glowed in the evening light. As we strolled, I sensed he was about to offer me a wonderful gift. I tingled with apprehension, knowing that the end of our walk would bring so much happiness. As I squeezed his arm in excitement, he looked down on me, his large frame towering over me. On my left, the garden of memories poured out its perfume. Large cabbage roses swayed, then changed colour and shape. Some were so large you could bury your face in them to absorb their energy and refresh yourself. I breathed in the pure air of love and instinctively breathed out the same vital air.

The next moment John and I were inside an incredible building. Rooms led off all around us, all with a sense of healing about them. Subdued colours enhanced the walls. The whole building made me feel good inside, like being held by a loving mother, safe, secure, and warm. John took me into a broad hallway as a feeling of expectancy built up inside me. I couldn't wait to enter the door in front of us. John introduced me to an Indian gentleman. His robes were gentle cream, his turban danced with lavender. He clasped his hands together in a greeting of respect, then led me to rows of baby cots where spirit babies lay fast asleep, waiting to descend to earth to their prospective mothers. The Indian gentleman walked a little way ahead of John and me. Turning with his arm outstretched, he pointed to a cot three down from the doorway. I tiptoed in case I awoke them all. Taking a deep breath and hardly daring to exhale, I stood at the foot of my grandchild's crib and gazed at the little bundle, snuggled down under a blanket soft as spider's thread.

'What will you be?' I wondered to myself, longing to know if it was a girl or a boy.

'Healthy!' John answered wisely, and he was right. The baby's health was far more important than its gender. Months later, we became the proud grandparents of a healthy Katie Jane. This amazing experience will stay with me forever. There can't be many grandmothers who have 'seen' their grandchild before it was born. This child and I have a special bond, different from my relationship with my other grandchildren, none of whom I visited before they were born.

My visit did not end there. I was taken to another wing of the hospital, which held those babies who had miscarried before birth. Without a doubt, miscarriage is one of the saddest human experiences. Perhaps because we had experienced this with Julie's first child, John and the Indian gentleman took me to see for myself those same babies who now lay wrapped in a golden material which mimics the mothers womb, soft, warm and loved, cocooned until they can progress and develop into beautiful and wise souls. The earth mother who miscarries has passed a difficult test of strength in this our earth school. Sometimes that test is one of decision, whether to carry on with or terminate the pregnancy. This is such a sensitive area and there is no single answer. An earth mother must understand that she may be forced to terminate her pregnancy, sometimes because it is impossible to carry on with it. She should not feel guilty over a decision which has been taken out of her hands. This soul has probably already progressed so far along its spiritual path that it just needs this last experience of being in a womb before it is allowed to progress to the highest realms. It will only return to the lower levels to welcome that mother when she also returns to the spirit realms, after a lifetime dealing with her own testing times.

It can be said that those mothers who lose babies before they are born were carrying angels. Such spirits are too special to stay in this world. These mothers are blessed by being allowed to carry such souls, even for a short time. They too are considered special by the spirit world. For these mums, there is a saying that may offer consolation,

'What God won't let you keep, he'll send.'

If we look at the spiritual side of events, we can begin to grasp the fuller meaning of the answers. It is when we search for answers only in the cold light of day that we are unsatisfied, because we look at it through physical eyes instead of spiritual eyes. This lifetime is but a blink in the process of a long road back to our spiritual home where all our loved ones are waiting for us.

Because this is such a sensitive area, I have chosen to cover a small portion of its wider implications. Of course if I tried to explain this painful area in greater depth, I would fill a book. I have tried with sensitivity to bring an under-standing to something that has eluded mankind forever. I do not claim to have all the answers, I just offer what I hope may help another on this path. The spirit worlds call our world ' the world of sorrow'. For some who lose children, that will not change. Others feel the presence of their children daily and siblings talk of other children seen around the home long after they have gone.

When my first marriage broke up, I needed to support my two children and myself so I took a job as a ward housekeeper on the children's wards of a local hospital. My responsibilities included making sure that everywhere was spotless and that the nursing staff had enough stocks of vital equipment. Although most of the patients were aged six or seven, one small baby lay alone in his own room. I knew he had a tumour growing inside his head, though there may have been other things wrong with him as well. Nothing could be done to help this child and his parents had found that visiting him was just too upsetting. I could easily understand that. Before I'd taken this job, I had never even thought about a child dying. Now I found it the most awful experience.

Although I knew his parents had been advised to just let him slip away and I could understand their absence from his bedside, it broke my heart that he never had any visitors. I got into the habit of starting each working day with a visit to his bedside. I'd drop in as often as I could during the day, too, on the pretence of cleaning his room, even though it was already spick and span. I couldn't bear to think of him alone there, thinking no-one cared enough to pop in and say 'How are you today, chubby chops?' I even thought he smiled at me quite a few times as I chatted to him while I worked, though that may have been a reaction to his illness.

Foolishly I assumed that no one had noticed that I had not taken any time off, not even holidays, since this mite arrived in the hospital. One day sister called me into her office and insisted that I took the next three days off. It was a wonderful weekend. The children and I spent Saturday at the beach, then tired and weary made our way home again at the end of a magical day. On Sunday after lunch, we went to the local park where we played until it was time for baths and bed.

After I reported to the ward next morning, I made straight for the baby's room. To my horror, I found it empty.

'He died quietly a few minutes after you left on Friday evening,' a nurse told me quietly. Her voice echoed in my head, sounding miles away. Tears welled up in my eyes as I turned away from her. 'It's all right, we all were upset when he passed away.' She put an arm around my shoulder in comfort. 'It's a part of the job which no one enjoys, especially when it's a child.'

That made my mind up. I was not prepared to see any more beautiful children slipping away and resigned the same week.

That was over 30 years ago but I never forgot the baby which wasn't mine but which I cared so much for. Even today, I wonder how tall he'd have grown, would he have had a happy life? I wondered whether he visited his earth parents often or if he'd moved on to more beautiful and spiritual heavens. Through my education I found my answers. That child and others like him are cared for and wrapped in the love of its soul family, who will cherish and love that child until an earth parent eventually joins them.

I wondered how parents coped with the loss of a child. John Redmond explained that parents of such a child needed to ask themselves this question. Try to look through your tears for your child, and recall not how your child died but what your child taught you while it was here. Was it love? Could it be patience, endurance, or greater thoughtfulness of others? Your child was an angel and here for a reason and you can be certain that those babies we have lost through death will know their parents on their own return to the spirit world. I wondered what happened to children who were abused and thrown into the spirit realms abruptly, often at the hands of their own parents. Surely such parents would not be reunited with these children. As always, John had the answer.

'These children are met and helped by those who do love them. Very soon they spend many hours in the company of a particular animal or bird which is a form of healing, very often for both souls.'

I know every parent who loses a child asks thousands of questions. If you have lost a dear child, I hope this chapter has gone some way towards answering some of those questions.

Chapter Thirteen

Spiritual healing

The subject of spiritual healing has always fascinated me. This is the ability to heal people of terrible afflictions, from headaches to a wide variety of painful disorders. The process allows spiritual energies to run from the crown of the head, through the palms of the healer's hands and then into the patient. I have always felt compassion towards fellow humans who suffer unimaginable pain and torment so I decided to join the ranks of the spiritual healer.

It was the worst day's work I have ever done. Oh yes, the healing energies flowed through my hands, each one displaying an array of wonderful colours, woven through with sprays of silver and gold flecks of light. But it was the after-effects which made me stop.

For several years, Keith my husband has had arthritis in his legs which is at times so painful that all I want to do is try to reduce the pain. One particularly bad day, I suggested he try healing.

'Who's going to give it to me?' he asked nervously.

'I will of course,' I confidently reassured him. As he lay on the settee, Keith began to tremble.

'Is the pain getting worse, love?' I enquired, concerned.

'No, what's worrying me is what you are going to do to me.' I ignored his sarcasm and very gently placed my hands a couple of inches above his body. Slowly as I felt the heat rising, I began massaging his feet, then moved upwards towards his painful knee. The heat from my hands became very strong, so much so that it began to hurt me. Worried, I stopped massaging, knowing that the heat shouldn't be painful for me. I glanced up at my poor husband.

'How are you?' I enquired. 'Feeling any better?'

'I'm not sure,' he answered. 'Have you finished? I think I'd rather have a cup of tea if it's all the same to you.'

'I think it's finished so I'll just wash my hands and put the kettle on. Nothing like a nice cup of tea to finish off the healing process, I'm sure.'

As the evening passed, the pain in Keith's leg grew steadily worse. I watched in horror as his knee swelled up to twice the size it should have been. Keith was in such pain that I insisted on calling out our doctor who came very quickly even though it was rather late. Neither Keith nor I mentioned my attempts at healing. After the doctor had given him a painkilling injection, Keith became more comfortable and was able to settle into sleep, though it took days for the swelling to go down.

I was more than disappointed. I'd really wanted to be able to cure him. But although I'd been confident that I could cure his painful arthritis, I had never actually promised that I would. Healing is not like that. No healer should promise a cure. We can only do our best, helped by the team efforts of the spirit worlds. Spiritual Healing needs no faith on the part of the patient. It can help animals or babies, just as much as adults. But I have learnt that some people cannot be healed, while others find great improvements in their health.

My next patient was quite surprisingly my daughter Samantha. When she was about sixteen, she began complaining of pains in the right side of her stomach. Months of back and fore to the doctor produced no improvement and no diagnosis, although she constantly cried with pain and was doubled over with the severity of it. One night when she had been particularly distressed, she shocked me by asking if I would give her some healing.

'You're joking,' I said amazed. 'After what happened to your father? I'll get the doctor.'

'Please, Mum,' Samantha cried, 'Couldn't you try first?' I put the phone down slowly and stared at her, thinking fast. Eventually I nodded.

'All right, but if it doesn't work, or you start to feel worse, I'm calling the doctor out straightaway. Understood?' She nodded eagerly and lay back onto the settee. I turned all the lights down so that the room felt soothing, then I drew the spirit realms close to me. I asked those in the worlds beyond to administer their healing love to my daughter in the safety of the Almighty. Suddenly there were electric currents in the air and small clouds of energy gathered around us. I was aware of a chill even though it was a warm and pleasant evening.

A man with something white draped around him came through a doorway from the unseen worlds. Standing only about five foot five, he told me he was Dr. Khan. He placed his hands together as if in prayer, then delved through Samantha's clothes and deep into the right side of her stomach. I watched wide-eyed as he brought out an illuminated ball.

'Are you all right, Sam?' I whispered.

'Yes, Mum,' she replied, 'But I can feel fingers inside my stomach, round about where the pain used to be. It's quite strange, this feeling, but I'm all right.' My eyes never left the glowing ball of light, very similar in size to a golf ball. Tenderly the doctor manipulated the ball before asking me to help.

'Please hold your hand over your daughter's stomach. I will then place this ball into your hands, after which you will please return it to my hands as quickly as you can.' Once it was back in his hands, he rolled it round, examining its shape and colour. Other spirits then closed around us to examine the still shining ball. Next, Dr Khan soothed Samantha's forehead, then slowly wiped her wound through her clothes. He bowed gracefully first to me, next to Samantha, then retreated through the door into the spirit world, taking the ball of light with him. I was transfixed as he and his student onlookers disappeared from the room. Suddenly I spun round, intent only on finding out how Sam had coped. She was lying peaceful and quiet on the settee cushions, seemingly asleep. I was just so thankful she seemed to be out of pain. I noticed again the distinctive aroma that I had first smelled in the room while Dr Khan was working on her. At last I could place it - anaesthetic. Sam had in effect had an operation.

I left the lights low and went out to the kitchen where I made a hot cup of tea for us both. I was on the edge of my seat, waiting for her to fully wake up and longing to know what she had experienced. Dreamily she stretched her arms over her head.

'That doesn't hurt now, Mum,' she said in wonder. I looked closely to see if there was any sign of the temperature she'd been running earlier in the evening but much to my delight, the harsh redness of her high temperature had faded into her normal healthy pink cheeks. But I was still concerned for her welfare and couldn't quite believe she was as well as she appeared to be.

'Perhaps we ought to get the doctor out, just to check you over,' I demurred.

'Oh, Mum, I feel great,' she announced. 'I have no pain at all. I just feel very good.' I poured her a cup of tea and passed it over to her.

'Did you actually see anything while you were lying down?' I asked, not wanting to put words into her mouth.

'No, not really,' she replied. She paused, then added hesitantly, 'I must have dozed off, I think, because I had this kind of dream that something or someone was moving around inside my stomach. I could feel what seemed like fingers searching around inside me but there wasn't any pain or discomfort. Then I felt something taken out of my stomach and there was a strong smell of that stuff they use in hospitals. I suppose I must have been a bit feverish.'

The following day there were no signs that there had ever been anything wrong with Samantha, or that any spirit doctors had come to call. That all happened about twenty years ago. Since then, Samantha has not complained of her stomach once. But she never forgot the whole thing. I must add that some years later she gave us two healthy grandsons, called Joe and Ben and the family were delighted.

Spirit people never cease to amaze me. I always feel humbled at their work and the way that they never let me down. Shortly after the episode with Sam, the same doctor from the spirit realms returned with a message for me. 'Take a short length of ribbon and hold your hands over it,' he instructed, his voice deep and positive. 'Think of me and others who have chosen to come closer to your world in the hope that we may heal those who ask for such help.' I kept such ribbons safe, offering them to anyone who might possibly benefit from their healing intentions, though I always made sure that I never guaranteed a cure.

I had a visit from a lady who was suffering from lack of sleep because she had a nervous disorder of the brain. I had no intention of attempting any healing upon her, instead I offered her a healing ribbon which she gratefully accepted. To my delight and I'm sure that of the spirit doctors, the lady's daughter wrote, explaining how well her mother had become after placing the healing ribbon under her pillow. The letter described the deep sleep the mother had enjoyed for the first time in many years, and as a result she had been able to begin to come to terms with her illness, which was the first step along the road to recovery.

Chapter Fourteen

Humour

The humour of the spirit world always seems to catch me out. Like all good comedians, the spiritual communities display their subtle wit and dry comments when the need arises; it's unexpected and very natural. I often look back and recall the more comical situations I have been drawn into or have fallen into without any help at all. I don't think many mediums can claim to have been a prize in a raffle. I was. And to add insult to injury, I was second prize. An angora wool cardigan was the first prize. What's more, I didn't even know I'd been offered as a prize until someone told me his sister had won me in the raffle. I had to laugh. I gave her a reading and never forgot my claim to fame.

'Whatever next, Tudor?' I giggled.

That episode was nearly as good as the time I advertised in the local paper to get my name more widely known. It was my mother who took the call. As she slammed down the phone, I could see she was ready to explode, her small round frame positively quivering with anger and her grey curls bouncing in indignation.

'What on earth have you said in your advert?' Mum enquired with a tone which would have melted an ice cap. I shrugged my shoulders.

Spiritual Medium, Readings, Messages offered.' My address, and of course my phone number.'

'I think you'd better check the paper,' Mum insisted, pushing it under my nose. I rustled through the paper until I found my advert. It sounded all right. As I passed it back to Mum, my eye caught the adverts above and underneath mine. They were for 'Massages'. I offered Messages. I thought my mother was going to faint, while I fell backwards over the settee, paper in hand, laughing till I choked. As I recovered, I mopped up my tears of laughter and tried hard to cheer my mother up after her shock.

'He'd have a shock if he found out what I do for a living,' I purred, grinning broadly and relishing the opportunity of a big send up. 'Shall I phone him back?' Funny how my mother's normally good sense of humour deserts her on occasions. Waiting for her eyebrows to meet in the middle when she's furious is not a pleasant sight. It's always the best time to grab a coat, fly out of the front door and duck down for a while. The man who phoned must have had a shock, inquiring how much I charged for a massage and what other services did I offer. Don't let anyone tell you that this work is for the gloom and doom brigade.

When David (I have changed his name for obvious reasons) came to see me, it was very difficult for him to open up to me straightaway. We talked about the weather and were making very little progress. Things changed when his late father made himself known to me.

Bill was David's old dad and had been in the spirit realms for a few weeks. He was quite different in shape and size, rounder and a little taller than his obviously nervous son. Bill beamed with confidence and, although I didn't know it at first, was a natural joker. His first words should have given me a clue.

'Tell your wife I love her but not enough to go to bed with her!' he chuckled, then gave the most outrageous laugh I have ever heard coming from the spirit world. Oh, boy, I thought, what have I got myself into this time? Just then, much to my relief, my old friend Tudor called in.

'What's going on, Tudor? Is this right?' Tudor nodded, smiling. 'Well, if you think so.' I raised my eyebrows and proceeded cautiously. 'I have a gentleman here. His name's Bill and he says he's your father.' I gave him some information which only David could have known.

'It must be my father,' said David. 'Only he knew that about me.' 'There is one other message he's asked me to pass onto you already.' I hesitated but Tudor had said it was all right so I took a deep breath and plunged straight in. 'He wants you to know he loves your wife but not enough to go to bed with her.' The silence stretched out endlessly. Almost too embarrassed by the message to look at David, I eventually plucked up the courage and glanced sideways at him. 'I'm sorry, I can only pass on what I'm asked to.' David smiled and I was puzzled to see relief in his face.

'Can I talk to him like you just did?'

'Of course,' I reassured him, 'Just ask your question and wait for your answer. Your father will tell me and in turn I will pass on what he says.'

'Well, Dad,' David shouted, cocking his head toward the ceiling. I automatically glanced up as well and winced.

'It's all right, David, your father can hear you. There is no need to shout.'
'That's exactly what I came here today to ask you about.' David ignored me, lowering his voice as he continued this extremely strange conversation.

'Would it be all right if I take you from under the bed, as Susan won't go into the bedroom until you're completely gone? In fact, Dad, she won't consummate the marriage until you're gone. Really gone, that is.' His voice was full of tears as he stretched out his hands to his father in supplication. By now, all my senses were on full alert! Talk about panic! It was a good job Bill knew the answer for I certainly didn't.

'That's OK by me, son, I really do understand.' The laughter had gone out of Bill's voice as he listened to his son's appeal. 'As long as you don't put me where I'll be forgotten.'

'I've given this a lot of thought, Dad, and wondered if it would be all right with you if I dug a patch at the bottom of the garden and placed you there?' By now, I strongly needed to understand where this conversation was going.

'Excuse me,' I intervened. 'Where exactly have you got your father and is he in a coffin?' I could hardly believe I was asking such questions but the conversation seemed to have got totally out of hand. I was becoming more and more worried and confused. I'm not a prude by any means but some standards must be maintained when dealing with the other side or all manner of rubbish can come through. David didn't seem unduly surprised at my intervention.

'When Dad died, we had him cremated, then put his ashes into a lovely urn. He and I were very close when he was alive and I couldn't bear the thought of putting the ashes somewhere he'd be on his own, so I kept them under my bed. Susan and I were meant to be spending our wedding night in our own home and that's when I told her where Dad was. Trouble was, she didn't understand at all. In fact, she got completely hysterical and now she refuses to go into the bedroom until I've moved Dad somewhere else.'

Trying to look serious in these sorts of circumstances is one of the most difficult parts of this work. I was dying to laugh but struggled hard to keep my giggles under control. After all, the matter was very serious to David. I could sense Bill hardly able to restrain his laughter as well, as he nudged me, then began gently teasing his son once again.

'I don't mind you putting me at the bottom of the garden but I'm a bit worried about the dog. What's to stop him lifting his leg over my new home?' But David had obviously realised this could be a potential problem and had the answer all worked out.

'Don't you worry about the dog. I'll put a wire fence around you and we'll plant a rose bush so it will look nice.' He hesitated, then lowered his voice again. 'Please let me do this, Dad. I miss you so much. This way, you seem to stay close to me.' Bill's emotion surged through me.

'You do that, son, it sounds very peaceful. If you can manage to broaden your mind a bit, Frances, I'd like to show you and David where I live now. It might help him to see I'm fine.'

David and I then saw Bill lying down in a cornfield, staring up at the spirit sky which rolled across like a tapestry of colour. Blues faded into rich lavender as the next kaleidoscope of pinks, lemons and pale greens blended across like a blanket of secure warmth. Flowers hung in droplets of crystal and nodded as beautiful coloured birds gracefully flew overhead. Nearby, the perfume of the garden of memories floated in a gentle breeze. Bill explained that walking in the garden and staring into a full rose head brought so many wonderful memories of his lifetime on earth. Bill has found peace.

Only Sixpence can, when she wishes, cause pandemonium, in the nicest way possible. She loves things which sparkle, so much so that she will borrow them for a while. I think she takes sparkling things because she never saw them when she walked the earth. She's by no means a kleptomaniac. They are often returned, but not necessarily to the right person or the right home. Several earrings of mine have vanished. I wouldn't mind so much but it's always one so I'm left with lots of single earrings. I often wonder who's got extras which don't belong to them. No one I have met has ever complained, they usually roar with laughter instead when they also have the Sixpence experience.

One day many years ago, a student in a class of mine asked about Sixpence. Sandra was a lovely happy soul who always found time to talk or laugh and she was fascinated by Sixpence's history. I explained how sometimes the child spirit is attracted to the most particular objects. It was as well I had warned her in advance, for, when I saw her next, she told me what happened after the class finished. It's a story I'll never forget.

After we'd said our goodbyes, my students returned to their homes which for Sandra meant quite a long drive up the motorway. After a light meal, she looked for her glasses, intending to watch some TV before going to bed. A swift search produced nothing so she upended her handbag on the floor. With a cry of triumph, Sandra pounced on her glasses case, then groaned as she realised it was empty. She sat back on her heels, trying to remember when she'd last had her glasses. She remembered looking at some photos at my house, so perhaps she'd pushed them into her coat pocket as she was leaving. But the pockets were as empty as the glasses case. With relief, Sandra remembered she'd thrown her coat onto the back seat of the car when she'd left my house, so perhaps the glasses had fallen out onto the floor of the car. But a thorough inspection of the car failed to find them.

Back in her living room, she pushed everything back into her handbag, picking up the glasses case last of all. She flipped open the case, unable to believe that the glasses weren't lurking in there somewhere. Suddenly something glinted in the corner. She prised it out and turned it over in her hands. A sixpence, a shiny brand new sixpence.

She laughed in delight as she remembered what I'd told her earlier that day about Sixpence's liking for shiny objects. Inspecting the coin more closely, Sandra was amazed to discover that it had been minted in 1950, the year of her birth.

When she told me the story, she was still tickled pink at finding that the spirit world could be so cheeky! But I couldn't stop apologising. Oh well, Sixpence is still my angel and I wouldn't swap her for all the tea in China. I haven't seen her wearing glasses yet but I'll bet she knows how to put her hands on a pair.

Several years ago, a radio which I'd been given as a Christmas gift went missing. I was convinced my sons knew more about its disappearance than they were letting on which made me so angry that, one very hot day, Samantha and I just argued non-stop. The atmosphere in the house was electric, we were really going at it, hammer and tongs. Our argument had nothing to do with the loss of the radio but I was just glad of the chance to get rid of some of my frustrations.

After all, radios don't just vanish into thin air, do they? Someone must have taken it. Not once did I suspect that the spirit realms had anything to do with its disappearance, until....

The argument I was having with Samantha was really beginning to get out of hand. We were both on the verge of saying things we would later regret, yet neither of us was prepared to stop. Suddenly a terrible noise reverberated close by, so loud that we stopped in our tracks and spun around, so startled that we clung to each other. A lampshade on the other side of the living room - a glass dome suspended on flex wire - was swinging wildly back and forth, nearly smashing on the ceiling from the force. We jumped again as a thunderous thud came from the adjacent dining room.

Neither of us wanted to investigate this new noise. Eventually Sam bravely plucked up the courage to go in and find out what had happened. I followed close behind her. I couldn't believe my eyes. On the table lay a metal cylinder with wires protruding from it. It was the inside of the radio, the one that had gone missing, the one I had blamed my sons for borrowing. It's my opinion that the spirit world had had enough of us all shouting and decided to do something to stop us. That, it definitely did!

Funny thing was Sam and I still do not know what we were arguing about but we did swear never to argue ever again. We dare not. Goodness knows what the spirit world would do to stop us next time.

In the late eighties, I was working in Cornwall at a meeting attended by Colin's mother. He had died after a long and difficult fight, leaving his mother grieving the loss of her only son. The day was full of sunshine and the atmosphere magical as I listened to the congregation singing in unison. I hummed along to the hymns, the words familiar but the tunes different from the ones we sang in Wales. Whether it was the warmth of the sunshine or the atmosphere I don't know but it wasn't long before the spirit world made their entrance.

A quiet voice beside me told me to look at the book of loved ones standing in pride of place on the podium with me. The thick heavily bound book stood open with photos adorning its contents. Each photo was followed by its own message of love. How lovely, I thought to myself, when out of the blue a young man stood next to me. He was without doubt a spirit and his beaming smile told me there was someone for him in the congregation. We had reached the part of the service which never fails to concertina my stomach, communication with the spirit realms. If I don't get that feeling, I know there is no-one close by from the spirit worlds. Delighted that the spirit world had turned up this day, I asked the young man whom he wanted to talk to. Bursting with love energy, he pointed.

'Do you see that lady there in the front row? That's my mother.' He gave me other information about his passing which I checked out with his mother before allowing him to go any further.

'That's my son,' she declared laughing loudly, happily agreeing to let me continue. The rest of the congregation enjoyed her evident happiness. The young chap was eager to impress his mother with his newfound spirit strength.

'Would you like me to convince you some more that it really is me?' he asked his mother.

'Yes please,' she answered enthusiastically.
'Do you see my mother's long gold earrings, Frances?' he giggled.

'Umm,' I answered, wondering what on earth he was planning to do. Before I could say anything else, his mother's earrings flew out of her ears and landed several rows back under a seat. As her ears were pierced, I winced at the thought of how much it must have hurt her but through tears of laughter, she told me it was wonderful and hadn't hurt a bit. In fact everyone said how amazing that service had been. I certainly enjoyed it, just as I had enjoyed many many others that took place over twenty years all over the country.

I well remember the time a musician came to see me. He had tried every single experience known to man except one.

'How can I have an out of the body experience?' he asked me. 'What if I tried some drugs? Would that do it?' He sounded quite frustrated at not yet having experienced this particular event.

'Yes, drugs should do it,' I confirmed. There was a long silence. 'Trouble is, there may be a problem with that.'

'Oh? What's that?' His eyes searched my face as the seconds ticked away on the clock. I really wanted to make him wait for my answer.

'You may not get back into your body the right way round,' I smiled sweetly. The look of utter terror on his face as he jumped up to leave convinced me he would abandon the project.

I remember a lady coming to see me many years ago. We had only just sat down when a gentleman came through. I asked him his name, then proceeded to ask him more personal things. I was amazed when he told me to mind my own business.

'That's between my wife and me!' he announced sharply.

'I'm so sorry,' I stuttered, red-faced, 'But he refuses to speak to me. I only asked him for some personal information and he told me to mind my own business.'

'Hurry up here and let's get home,' he said gruffly to his wife. 'It's nearly supper time.'

With that, off he went. The lady smiled as contented as a Cheshire cat.

'If you gave me my husband any other way, it wouldn't be him,' she explained. 'I wanted to know that he was as miserable as me. Without him moaning all the time, it's boring. Now I'm happy because you've let me know he's missing me. He hasn't changed a bit, the old sod.'

With that, she made her way to my front door, still smiling. None so queer as folk.

Chapter Fifteen

Past Lives

Throughout the chronicles of this way of life, each event seems to outsmart or outdo the last. So it would be ridiculous at this stage not to include a bizarre episode I was fortunate to observe first hand some years ago during the '80s.

Mother and I had travelled to the historic city of Bath at the invitation of the Spiritualist Church there. It was always a pleasure to work in this particular church, which was well attended by considerate and hospitable people willing and ready to learn. The church stood dwarfed by the mighty buildings of this fascinating city, which, steeped in tradition, was a maze of streets leading to one of the finest cathedrals in the country. People from all over the world arrive en masse to see, feel and generally experience its magnificent traditions. History is everywhere in the grand old city of Bath so it seemed only natural to expect some interaction with the past while we were there. We were not to be disappointed.

We had arrived a little early and, with time to spare, meandered towards the Spiritualist church. Even so, we arrived before we were expected. The sun warm on our faces, Mum and I chatted as we waited patiently for the secretary to open the church so we could settle down, unpack our weekend clothes, and check out the times of the evening services. Everywhere was quiet. No music came from the surrounding apartments, no clatter of dishes from the nearby restaurants. Silence. A breeze cooled our faces every now and again. I was thinking how good a cup of tea would taste right then and hoped we wouldn't have to wait much longer for one.

Suddenly I recognised it. A stillness, so familiar to me as a medium, surrounded me. A nerve fluttered in my stomach, my throat became dry. Something was stirring in the atmosphere, building to a climax. The air was electric all around me, the day different, expectant. Beside me, my mother's voice chatted on about all manner of everyday things. I could hear her but it was as if she were a thousand miles away. I took a deep breath and looked down the old cobblestone road. What was that I could hear? The noise of movement, solid, a clattering, but not of dishes or something tinny from nearby restaurants. I tensed in anticipation. Suddenly I knew what it was – the clattering of horse's hooves hitting cobblestones. I shook my head slightly but it was definitely a horse, trotting towards me. I could hear it but I couldn't see it. What in the name of common sense was happening?

Mum noticed the expression on my face as I stared at the other end of the cobblestone road. I was speechless, unable to say what I was seeing. Through a doorway in time, I could 'see' another dimension imprinted on the present. Locked in time, I stood at the doorway to the past.

'What are you looking at, Frances? Tell me,' Mum appealed. She turned to look briefly down the same road as me, then looked back at me. 'There's nothing there, Frances.'

'On the left hand side of this road,' I explained without taking my eyes off the vision. 'I can see a coach and horses. They're coming toward us. No! They've stopped. Can't you see them too?'

'No.' I felt so disappointed that she was missing this glorious sight. Needing to share the scene unfolding before my eyes, I described every detail to my mother.

'The horse is black, standing tall and proud. I can't see the driver clearly. He's holding the reins and sitting on the front of the black carriage.' Then a veil came down between my vision and me and they were gone. No, they had just vanished for a second. 'They've stopped outside the doorway of that large building at the end of the road. A gentleman's stepped down from the carriage. Oh, how grand he looks. Black top hat and snow white gloves, with a cape thrown over one shoulder. He's stretching a hand up to the door of the carriage and helping down a lady. She's so graceful. She's wearing a long evening gown, dark in colour but pretty and very expensive. There's a stole loosely wrapped around her slim shoulders, her hair's swept up on her head under what seems to be a decoration on top of her dark hair.' Almost too excited to explain any more to my mother, I could see that the couple were walking into the large building. Then I heard a name. Sara! 'This lady is so special, Mum. She's very famous and something to do with the theatre. I know it's in the past, I just can't work out how long ago.'

The scene faded. I was back in the present at the end of the cobble-stone road. But nothing was going to stop me finding out where they had gone. With my heart in my mouth and my stomach churning, I abandoned our bags and curiously walked up to the doorway through which my vision had disappeared. Although it had gone from my sight, it was locked in, recorded on my mind. Once I'd reached the door, I couldn't believe what I had found. Excitedly, I called Mum to hurry up. Puffing and panting, she soon stood by my side. On a plaque erected on the outside wall of the large building, I read:

'Opened in 1750, the Theatre Royal. For four years between
1778 - 1782 the building was used for acting, making it home to some
of the greatest names in theatre.'

Then my eyes grew larger as I read:

'The celebrated actress, SARAH SIDDONS, made her appearance
within those four years.'

The notice also told us that the Theatre closed down in 1805. This was the first time I had ever heard of the Theatre Royal or indeed of Sarah Siddons.

I felt giddy with the whole experience, and so excited. My journey to the past had obviously taken place between 1778 1782. Wildly, my mind jumped between knowing that I was actually in the 1980s, yet my mind had forged backwards into history. Somehow I had sparked off a psychic experience of such proportions that a scene from over two hundred years ago had been brought to life. I felt indeed privileged to be a witness to such an amazing vision belonging to the past.

My only problem lay with the fact that I had heard the name 'Sara', yet Sarah Siddons spelt her name with an 'h'. I mentioned this to a friend who supplied what may be the answer to the mystery, at the same time as lending credence to my vision. Sarah Siddons was born in Brecon at a time when it was strongly Welsh-speaking. In those communities, 'Sarah' was pronounced 'Sarai', like 'Sar' with 'eye' on the end. It's entirely possible that, in my bemused state at seeing this vision, I heard 'Sarai', yet my mind, not knowing of this pronunciation, heard 'Sara'.

This experience made me wonder if life is similar to a simple video recording, if everything said and done is recorded in the ether. Just one event may open this video recording. It could be the heat from the sun, a person with extra abilities, psychic or spiritual, or a combination of both. Then again, it may be something else entirely. Records have shown that people without any psychic or spiritual gifts have opened doors to the past, reliving battles or witnessing troops of Roman soldiers, marching along. There does not seem to be any logic to these occurrences, just the knowledge that it happens.

To be a spectator at a doorway to the past is most odd. I tingle, shake with anticipation of what will be shown as the door opens. My heart beats fast, my breath is drawn in sharply. My eyes prepare to witness everything, no matter what that should be. It's most unusual for a person to have this journey to the past once in a lifetime. Yet it has happened to me twice. The second time I had this experience turned out to be so grisly that I have decided I might close my eyes in any future visions.

The second episode of viewing the past came when I was taking a service in South Wales. The small town sitting in the valleys was of no special historical importance that I knew of. The building, rented for a few pounds a week, was clean and held enough chairs to accommodate the growing congregation. The service was in mid swing. The hymns, sung with the enthusiasm of a Welsh choir, were long over. I had reached the part where I was offering messages from loved ones in the spirit world to recipients in the congregation.

I had just finished talking to a lady and it was time to connect with someone else from the spirit realms. Suddenly through the door of the building came a workman, followed quickly by another man. Between them they carried a third man on a stretcher. All three looked equally dirty and tired. I watched as the stretcher-bearers rushed past me, turning the corner of the hall and walking hurriedly down a narrow passage into another room. The door was ajar. I was able to see briefly a line of temporary beds. This was repeated, as another set of men carrying injured people dashed past me. Then it happened a third time.

I described everything in detail to the congregation. Everyone was as mystified as I was. No one could shed any light on what I was talking about.

How could these people run down a passageway that wasn't there, how could anyone go through a brick wall? Everyone talked of the mystery. Eventually one elderly lady recalled her parents telling her, as a child, that another building had once stood on the same spot. That building had a passage running down to a room. Her mother had told her that some sort of mining disaster had occurred many years before and they'd used that room to put the injured on stretchers. My knowledge is scant on such matters but some years later a friend discovered by accident that, in 1890 a mining disaster actually did take place in or around the area where I was narrating my vision. The fatalities were in the region of 200 with many severely injured being brought out of the mine as well.

Fortunately I don't experience these visions as much as I used to. Not all spirits will take notice of a medium, or anyone else, and insist on causing as much trouble as possible for as many people as they can. No amount of persuasion will move them from their activity, happily plodding on without any urge to move forward. It's well documented that some people hear Roman soldiers, marching in unison along familiar routes unaware of the dramatic changes of time. Even those on the battlegrounds of the first and second world wars can be unaware that another life awaits them, one filled with hope, peace and meetings with long-gone loved ones. It is so sad that, through their upbringing, many were taught that it was silly to believe in a spirit world.

Even as you read this page, there are people lost on this earth, because they have no belief or spiritual understanding. However, not everybody who returns to the spirit world is so ignorant today, thank goodness. Loved ones, gone on before, meet them and embrace one another once again.

Chapter Sixteen

My American adventure

My American adventure began totally unexpectedly while I was working in Cardiff City, which is in South Wales in the United Kingdom. Yes, unexpected things do happen to psychics too. A group of people asked if they could film my work.

"But why?" I asked. Questioning motives is part of the makeup of a Welsh person.

"Because, my dear," one of the group answered, "You are to be famous!" That took the wind out of my sails and I began laughing. My laughter infected one after the other in the large group until, with the speed of light, everyone was convulsed with mirth. The lady who'd made the wild claims smiled and stood up.

"I'm sending this video tape to Nevada USA," she said, taking a deep breath. She stared into my eyes to see what my reaction would be. The laughter drained out of me and for once, I was at a loss for words. "You must go as well. You're needed in the States, you and your Angels."

To this day, I don't know what I said for the rest of the evening. I couldn't understand why I should be needed overseas. After all, the United States has some of the finest mediums in the world. What could I add to them? Just what did the Spirit Team have up their sleeves for me now?

A week later, I answered the phone one afternoon.

"Hello, my name's Christine," said a voice calmly. "I live in Nevada and want to invite you to come visit us." My heart beat faster.

"Just when were you thinking of?" I asked faintly, visualising my commitments for the following year.

"How about six weeks' time?"

Silence. Never in the history of the telephone can it have been so quiet. Two women on the phone and not a word between them. That's got to be a world record. Eventually I broke the silence.

"All right," I answered, before I could think of the thousand reasons there had to be for not going. Just how could I arrange everything in such a short space of time, anyway? I was due to work in London. But I was not going to work in London, I was going to America instead.

I couldn't have been more excited if I tried. In the weeks leading up to my departure, I would often retire to the garden with my newspaper in one hand, a mug of coffee in the other, and wonder just what was in store for me.

One Sunday afternoon I planned to do just that, relax in the garden for a while. I'd worked hard all summer cultivating my small patch and it had rewarded me by being filled to the brim with English roses of all colours and perfumes. I sat down on the garden bench and relaxed, breathing in the wonderful scents around me. Gradually, I became aware of a stillness in the air on that warm summer day. Life slowly ground to a simmer and a familiar silence filled the air as the normal clatter of an Industrial town faded into serenity around me.

My stomach churned wildly. I had learned a long time ago that this meant I was in the presence of a spirit which had not long left this world. Angel guides were near, bringing with them a young soul. My eyes moved to the centre of the silence a few feet away from me. A spirit figure appeared through this vortex of energy, an airman's peaked cap slightly hiding his strong very young features. I sat bolt upright, my attention completely focused on him. My newspaper cascaded unnoticed onto the path. Fully intent on this young spirit, I watched and waited, oblivious to where I was. My heart raced. A cascading array of glorious colours exploded round him like fireworks in slow motion but without their loud harsh noises. Gently, gracefully he moved toward me, folding into and through a breathtaking display of love energy. I felt so humbled by his presence and his powerful strength as he tilted his handsome face slightly, a smile on his lips. I looked into eyes filled with love, sparkling as he looked deep into mine. I felt my throat dry while our eyes locked together for what seemed an age but was only a silent moment.

My heart went out to him. Emotionally I felt his sadness and tears welled up in my soul. Pain, not the pain that took his life but the pain of his grief, swept over him and me like a dark cloud passing the sun. Part of my mind registered that his uniform was different from that of my own country's air force. Taking a deep breath I began to speak to him but there was no need. He spoke softly with his mind directly into my mind, his American accent coming through loud and clear.

Slowly, mentally, he showed me images. Back home, his home, America. A large lady, crying bitterly, rocked in a chair, a small white handkerchief held tightly in her hand. The airman indicated that the sorrowing lady was his mother, grieving bitterly for him. Other people were present, all family members and all bearing the same grief.

"You will tell her I'm OK, won't you ma'am?" he whispered solemnly. I just nodded. He smiled gently. I felt in place of his grief a powerful pride and a sense of adjustment to his death. As quietly and unobtrusively as he'd arrived, so he slowly vanished.

I sat for a long time, wondering about the significance of the visit and what the spirit realms had set up for me now, but I soon realised that a very special American airman needed help, which I intended to deliver for him. I felt honoured to be chosen for that task.

But what chance was there of ever meeting this young man's family? After all, not everyone knows about mediums and their work. Besides, how big is Las Vegas? Was his family even from there or were somewhere else in America? Most importantly, I couldn't go to them, they had to find me. I didn't know how or where to start finding them, I didn't even know their names or for that matter whether they wanted to see a medium. How would they set about this task of searching me out at the precise time I would be available? Already the cards were stacked against any meeting. I felt so sorry for them all. Maybe a little prayer would help, I thought.

I sat back in my chair, the sun gently warming my face, then smiled quietly to myself as the obvious struck me. If 'they' needed me to bring this family together from the two worlds, it would require nothing short of a miracle. But I knew full well the spirit world was good at miracles and this young man would not have visited me unless moves were already afoot for that miracle to happen.

The memory of this short event stayed in my mind. On the flight to Nevada, I shared the experience bit by bit with my mother so that no one could accuse me later of making up the elaborate story. I wondered, while I peered out of the window of the plane, if the young airman had begun his long task of getting his family to book me. I did hope so. Meanwhile I thought it best to put it out of my mind and let the spiritual forces get on with their work.

I didn't have to wait long for things to start happening. Within a few short days of my arrival, the phone rang and I was asked to visit a family who desperately needed the services of a medium. Mum and Christine, who was my Las Vegas host, came with me. The house was like nothing we have over here in Britain, seemingly built on several levels.

"Hi, I'm Paul. Welcome to my home," said the young man who greeted me on my arrival. "I'm the one who phoned you. I'm hoping you can help my mother." He reminded me of someone but I just couldn't put my finger on the memory. We went into the living room where hoards of children raced around. Paul shooed them away and led me towards the far corner where a lady sat in a chair.

"Mom, this is the medium from the UK. I told you about her, remember?" As she turned towards me and I saw her clearly for the first time, I gasped. It was the same lady the young airman in my garden had shown me mentally. His vision was completely accurate. Her large frame rocked as she wept for her dead son.

"She's been like this since my brother died," explained Paul, who was obviously 'my' airman's brother. "I'm afraid we don't know what to expect from you. We've never had any contact with a medium before but Mom's getting so upset that we'll try anything." He shooed away two small children who were trying to climb onto his mother's lap. "Would you like somewhere quieter to do whatever it is you have to do?"

I nodded and Mum, Christine and I followed several members of Paul's family down to a quiet room in another level of the house where I went to work. I was so determined to do everything possible for this family and their beloved son. The same young air force man came through. He spoke to Paul, giving him masses of information about how he'd died, the name of his commanding officer, and the problems he'd had with his health, although his family knew nothing of this. Mother sobbed quietly, as her late son described various items Paul had now inherited from his brother. However, I soon became aware of a certain unease in the room and looked questioningly at Paul.

"This is all fine," he said, squirming slightly. "And I don't mean to say we don't believe you but we knew none of that information before so cannot rightly say that you are telling us something which is really coming from my brother. Is there any way you can prove to us that my brother is really talking to you?"

My airman was aware of this need to convince his family without question that he was really there at that particular moment.

"There's a brown holdall, with a letter for Mike up in the cupboard," he whispered to me. "It's in the next room. That was my bedroom when I was alive. Go get it." He yelled the last piece of information at me so suddenly that I nearly fell off my chair.

Paul looked surprised when I relayed this instruction to him. "I checked out that room," he protested. "There's nothing there, we cleaned it all out after the funeral."

"Tell him to get the bag. Go look!" insisted the airman, becoming frustrated. Paul and I duly went into the next room which held very little furniture, so it didn't take long to find the brown holdall up and at the back of the tall cupboard out of sight.

"I searched my brother's belongings. This wasn't there then," whispered a stunned Paul, swallowing hard. He grasped the holdall between his hands, turning it over and over in disbelief. Then he raced back into the other room where the rest of the family waited silently for us.

"The bag," he announced limply to his white-faced family. "There really was a bag there. This is weird, man."

My spirit friend wasn't finished yet, as he was determined to convey to his family just how easily he could communicate with them.

"Look inside, there's a letter for Mike," he advised his brother. Paul held the bag open and looked inside, turning out various pockets in his search.

"Mike was an old friend of my son's," explained a tearful Mom, speaking for the first time. Sure enough, the astonished Paul brought out a letter. As Paul read the contents of the letter out loud, my spirit friend told me word for word what it said, a little ahead of his astonished brother, so that I could 'read' it in unison with Paul.

"It's for 'Mike'," whispered Paul, handing it round for everyone to inspect. The family looked at me uneasily. The air had turned cold and the atmosphere filled with trepidation. Someone commented in a whisper on the grey misty cloud that had built up around us, which I knew the spirit realms needed in order to move in closer and stronger than before.

"How did she know?" I heard whispered round the room. A wave of fear began to envelop the room. I could not allow this to happen, it would take the beauty out of the sitting. Understanding his family's shock, the airman proceeded to prove to them that although he was out of sight, he still spent quite a lot of time at home amongst his family. He was very much aware of his demise but that wasn't going to stop him!

"Watch this!" he whispered to me. I just had time to prepare myself for the next bombshell. Much to the delight of Paul and the rest of the family, more private family matters came tumbling from my lips, together with information on situations and events of which I couldn't possibly have had any knowledge. The spirit of the airman was in full swing as tales of family life were exchanged. Enjoyment and amazement were present in equal measure as memories jogged other memories. Around us tears fell as happiness and relief washed over grief.

Then my special talent came into play. I have an unusual ability to allow spirit loved ones to touch their Earthly family, one another, just feather-light touches, but nonetheless quite distinct. The young airman walked over to members of his family, just touching an arm or head gently or brushing against shoulders. Cries of "Wow" and "Did you feel that?" followed excitedly. Some felt tiny shivers run down their arms as the young airman gently touched them one by one.

Mom stopped crying. Instead she began repeating, "Oh my God," over and over, her large handkerchief falling down at her side, her eyes almost protruded from their red rimmed sockets.

"It's him, it's my boy," she declared loudly, laughing and crying at the same time. "He's home with me again. My baby, my baby. Thank you, God."
The atmosphere had again changed. The family burst into sudden laughter at the prospect of communication. The subdued lighting now seemed bright as if a cloud had been swept away as I looked around at the happiness of a family reunited.

The young airman that had first come to my country with his request was here with his loved ones, just as he wanted it. Again and again, he touched each one present, then as if to say 'thank you', he drew himself over to me. I tingled when he gave me a hug and let him carry on. This was his time with his loved ones, I was just glad to witness first hand another person in spirit who could now carry on with his new life in the spirit realms. I suppose he had the best of both worlds, able to live over there and visit loved ones here when he was ready to.

A man engineered all this with the assistance of others in a spiritual world. He had "died" some months before, yet he'd made it his business to visit me in my country so that through my work, his family could carry on with their lives instead of grieving.

I wondered why he needed me. There are after all some very fine mediums in the world, many in America. I have often thought that it may have been because of my ability to stretch my aura, allowing spirit loved ones to touch once again. What a thrill it must be for them. What's particularly intriguing is trying to work out how he knew I was going to the USA and his hometown in particular. I assume "they" must communicate with one another. The spirits truly do work in mysterious ways and always work to bring happiness into the lives of those who grieve. There is always a feeling of satisfaction when a first class communication is held and everyone benefits because of it.

The time I spent in America brought me in contact with the most in-credible array of people and their lifestyles. I will always have a soft spot for them all. I love the Americans and their wonderful country, but when I strolled into a store in the mall, I was asked if I came from Britain.

"Yes," I replied.
"What part? Is it England?" sang the excited query.
"No, Wales", I replied.
"Oh!" she drawled limply, "I've always wanted to go to Scotland."

I didn't bother to explain. I just rolled my eyes to my companion and smiled, leaving as quickly as possible before I embarrassed anyone with my giggles. What lovely people the Americans are, and they call us quaint!

The American Indian is without doubt one of the most gentle of human races. Throughout history they have held our imagination like no other could. Their gentle way of life reflects on prayers to the Great White Spirit, and, combined with the most spiritual uplifting messages, shows us all how to live. Over time the British medium has regarded the American Indian as one of the most spiritual of races. Their spiritual rituals are as famous as any known to Man.

From birth Native Indians are taught the simple facts of the spirits and how to communicate with them. When the Indian returns to the spirit realms, he often returns to mediums as a guide or carer. We could learn so much from their teachings and simple way of life.

So imagine how I felt when I was invited to the reservation of the Nevada Indian. This would be the epitome of my spiritual career. Me, Fran Hollis-Powles, going to the homeland of all that is considered spiritual.

I had the advantage of meeting a lovely lady by the name of Nancy who ran her own film and audiotape company in Las Vegas. One of her projects was a documentary of the famous Paiute tribe. As a favour to me, she managed to arrange a meeting with the spiritual leader of this tribe on the reservation. My heart beat faster and faster at the news, which was particularly exciting as normally the Paiute tribe do not allow contact with anyone not of their race.

Mum and I had to meet Nancy at her business address. So Christine, the girl we were staying with while we were in Las Vegas, drove us there. We arrived as the sun was going down. Excitement was boiling over in me. After changing from Christine's car into Nancy's, we had been travelling some time in total darkness out into the desert when I spotted a sign saying, Reservation. I tried hard to cope with my enthusiasm at the thought of meeting an American Indian face to face, though in fact I was bursting with excitement at the prospect.

It was quite a while before we stopped outside a general store which sat next to a few homes belonging to these spiritual people. Nancy got out of the car and disappeared into the store. I peered through the windows of the car in the hope that maybe a member of this community would pass by but no one came near.

I decided to get some goods from the store while we were waiting. As I clambered out of the car, Nancy called to me. My eyes nearly popped out of my head for there in front of me stood, at only four foot and a spit, a lovely warm-looking woman with the unmistakable proud features of her tribe. Her grey hair tumbled down her back, as she made a move toward me in a gesture of a hug. My mouth dropped open in awe of this lady. I hope that my surprise at this wonderful greeting didn't upset her in any way, for, as she came forward, I stepped back in absolute shock. I wanted this moment to last forever, I was so chuffed. Or thrilled, I should say.

We all got into the car and another drive took us to what seemed to be a nursery school. We were still on the reservation and my happiness did not falter. Every move this lady made I watched. Every word she spoke I listened to earnestly. We settled down on the tiniest chairs I've ever seen and I watched as her ancestors drifted around her. Their ghostly heads stretched this way and that as they looked round at everything. These spirit folk were as tiny as their great great-grand daughter. All her family turned up, as interested in me as I was in her and them.

In her small-framed face I could see long lines of her ancestors. She held her head high as her long grey hair fell down her back. No more than 4ft 11ins, this lady embodied all I had dreamt of as one who trod the old road of spiritual enlightenment. Hugs galore, she wrapped herself around me in greeting. My head spun with excitement of what was in store that evening.

The following hour or so brought people from her immediate past, as she explained her work briefly in the sweat lodge, which involved visions and trying to work her way toward helping others in healing. Already surprised that a female was the spiritual leader of the tribe, I was even more wide eyed at the news that she did not work in a psychic way. It was me who lunged into a reading as this lovely lady sat down with me, inside what seemed to be a community building.

I described her long-deceased family as they drew closely around her. They looked smaller than she did. I was deep into the reading when a young man entered the room. After she'd introduced him as her son, he sat alongside me, watching, listening. From then on, the reading became difficult, as he seemed indifferent to me. The difficulty increased until I began giving more of a spiritual reading of his direction in life, of where and how he would gain insight into why he was here on earth, his spiritual pathway, if you like. The reading was eventually successful, I was sure. He thanked me and rose up from his seat. We said our farewells and travelled back to the town where I was staying.

I thought hard about why this young man was so hostile in his manner. He'd asked me why did I have the gift, what had I done to deserve it? He knew that when the spiritual reading began I was working with spiritual advice from the ancestors, his ancestors. Anything before that was from my psychic abilities. He would not accept any less than that and I would have been a fool to think he would. He wanted quality not quantity.

I kept the audiotape of that meeting. Who would believe that a white British woman could give a reading to an American Indian?

As a treat, my mother and I were invited to a Pow-wow of many tribes, while we were staying in Nevada. I was ecstatic at the prospect of walking and talking to more of those great people. The stalls, arranged in a circle, displayed everything you would expect from the different tribes. War bonnets lavishly decorated in beautiful coloured feathers, amazing Indian blankets of many patterns, jewellery of intricate designs. I walked round and round the circle of culture, completely dazzled by the incredibly high standard of everything I saw. The meaningful dances were full of traditional values. My head was filled with the excitement of the day. How many times had I heard that the spirit worlds produce a rare treat for a medium they are particularly pleased with? And this was to me the highlight of my trip.

I was in the middle of purchasing an audiotape of music played by members of these wonderful people who understand more of deep spirituality than most when the man who was selling me the tape asked where I had come from.

"Britain," I answered, almost in a whisper.
"What part?"

"Oh, Wales," I smiled, wondering if he knew where that was in Britain. Many do not. I searched his face for a history of the old ways. My romantic visions were suddenly reduced to hysterical laughter.

"Llanfairpwllgwyngyllgogerychwyndrobwllllantysilioggogogoch," he intoned solemnly.

"Congratulations," I replied, my eyes streaming with tears of laughter. Here was I from Wales and couldn't even pronounce the 'gogogoch' without crossing my eyes.

That was an extremely wonderful day. I met and spoke with people I never thought in a million years would show so much of the old ways to a stranger like me. My heart missed a beat so many times that day. The sky melted from reds into gold as the day ended and shadows stretched unending. I was truly blessed.

One of the teaching weekends I gave in America resulted in me working while everyone else relaxed. All my helpers had been working so well and we had all become such good friends in the process, that I decided to give them a treat. I had already tuned in to all the helpers and guides, theirs and mine, to ask for their help. The guides had asked me to do them the courtesy of requesting their help before any work was carried out with them. After all, it was only common courtesy. Who would turn up anywhere, if not invited? I know I wouldn't.

I called to Sixpence, my little spirit helper, for her help in a familiar exercise. Everyone gathered round in a horseshoe shape, seated on anything they could lay their hands on, while the spirit realms and I built up sufficient energy to expand the aura surrounding me. This is like butterfly wings stretching out enough to allow spirit loved ones to touch once again.

This particular session was going well until a special friend needed to give his love to a delightful young lady called LeJanne. As I called her over, her long hair shone in the little light of the room as her slim frame and pretty smiling face searched eagerly for what delights the spirit realms were to offer her.

"Come closer, love, and kneel down to my right side." I requested. LeJanne hesitated.

"It'll be all right," I reassured her. She glanced over her shoulder to her friends and shrugging her shoulders, did as I'd asked. Immediately she was pushed over by the wet tongue of her beloved spirit dog from the spirit realms. I was quite relieved when I'd called her over, as her dog was quite large and had been leaning heavily against me with his great bulk. Her laughter filled the air as she rolled from side to side under his weight. The onlookers watched in amazement as the smell of a dog just coming in from the rain permeated the large room. Laughter and love by the bucketful made everyone join in. Tears filled the air as owner and pet exchanged kisses.

"I can feel him, I can actually feel him," squealed a delighted LeJanne. She was so overwhelmed by the experience that no one was surprised to see what we thought were tears of happiness running down her pretty face. But when we looked closer, we could see her face was wet from the tongue of her darling dog. Large slobbering licks had drenched her face, but she didn't care. One of her favourite dogs was back and as happy as his mistress. His tail wagged enthusiastically, whipping me as he eagerly washed her again.

So much love passed between them, I don't think there was a dry eye in the room. There certainly were a great deal of "oohs" and "ahhs" that day, I can tell you. I will let you into a secret. That was the first time a dog had come through like that. Hope it's not an elephant next time.

There is a great deal of satisfaction helping spirit people and animals gain that special bond again. I know it is only for a short time but the help it brings can shorten the grieving pattern considerably, so surely that can't be such a bad thing, can it?

I have taken the opportunity of talking to some informative guides to find out what happens to animals once they pass over. Obviously ones like LeJanne's dog seem to enjoy a wonderful life in the spirit world. Many an animal is met by an owner or carer after the transition, someone who shows them that they must not be afraid, that a whole meadow or field is theirs to roam freely under the spirit sunshine, where others whom they were familiar with can join them. Family pets greet their owners with the cheeky playfulness of past times, when the owner returns to the spirit world. No more partings because of death, just time to be together again, enjoying each other's company. In fact every four-and two-legged friend who roams on this earth survives, just as we do, in the spirit worlds. All, including birds, are treated with respect and tons of love.

I once was asked if animals in the spirit worlds could talk. My answer is, yes. Your cat or dog has ways of letting you know when they need feeding or to go out. What they don't do is speak as we do. If they could talk on earth, then they would be able to speak in heaven. I know of many spirit animals that let me know that their owners are close by. They wag a tail or make a noise but they do not speak.

But not all animals have such a good life on earth. Those animals that sadly are driven to the slaughterhouse are on different levels from humans, and are cared for by Angel children who do not know what earth life is like. They never have been to earth and have no knowledge of malice or pain. I was told that no human contact is made again with these animals, unless a soul is so progressed that it is able to reach out to these poor souls and gain their confidence.

If all you ever wanted while on earth was to take care of horses or any other animal, and for many reasons were not able to, the opportunity can arise when you're in the spirit realms. It's up to you, and your attitude and how you fare in this life are very important. There are those of us who are only happy in the company of animals, they simply do not like human contact. They are the ones who make the best carers of all animals, so they obviously make their own heaven, and a special healing takes place between human and animal. One helps the other to understand their demise.

Sixpence, my guiding child angel, repeated a name over and over - Bill. "Bill who?" I'd ask inquisitively. She'd giggle again and whisper 'Bill.' I gave up asking and forgot about it. If this Bill chap was going to call, he'd be as welcome as anyone else.

One day near the end of my stay in America, I received a phone call from a film director.

"I've been hearing a lot about your special talents," she said, after introducing herself. "I'm at the airport catching a flight to Las Vegas at this moment. I'm on my way to a very important interview but I'm hoping you can fit me in beforehand?" I worked out that I could just squeeze her in before my own flight home.

Twenty minutes later, she phoned back.

"I'm not going to be able to make it after all," she told me, disappointed. "That interview I mentioned? Well, it's with Bill Clinton, you know, the President? And they've just phoned to reschedule it. So I'm not going to have time to see you, I'm afraid."

"Oh! That Bill," I gasped. "Well, I daresay I could fit you both in, if you like!" Never mind, there'll always be a next time.

My new American friends did so much for me while I was in the States. Christine got in touch with the Spiritual Endeavours Centre where they offer all kinds of alternative and complementary therapies. They agreed to send out to people on their mailing list pamphlets which Christine designed and had printed for me. These pamphlets seemed to travel far and wide across America and ended up with all sorts of people. Consequently I ended up giving readings to people from as far away as Chicago and New York, well beyond the Centre's areas of influence. People even turned up on our doorstep from places like Philadelphia and Maryland. I did all kinds of work in Las Vegas – stage presentations, individual readings, teaching weekends. What is particularly gratifying is that I still hear from many of those I was in contact with during this first visit, contact which has been made so much easier recently with the introduction of emails.

Of all the people I met during this time, one became of particular interest to me. Dr. Barbie was a charming authoress of international status. I will not of course divulge her reading, but her delight with what I told her led to me being granted the auspicious title of one of the world's best mediums. A gentleman in Florida told me of this amazing accolade when he rang me to ask for a reading. He had previously phoned Dr Barbie to ask for the services of a reputable medium and she had told him about me. I went on to find that a millionaire had hired Dr Barbie, who became my friend. For three years Dr Barbie was to investigate mediums and find out the genuine ones. The result was my illustrious title of one of the world's greatest mediums. Plain old Frances Hollis-Powles. I didn't think I was anything special, just doing a job with special friends at the helm. But if we have made someone's life change for the better, then we are just doing what we are here to do and that has got to be good.

Just before I heard the news, I was back home and cleaning the cooker, so if anyone had seen 'one of the world's best mediums' at that moment, she was wearing her husband's old socks, trousers and a floppy jumper. What a star!

Naturally I am flattered and quite bedazzled by the whole thing. In fact the feeling I experienced almost matched the happiness I felt at being in the company of those wonderful people in America, who are never far from my mind and heart.

I was sad to leave the States. The whole experience had been so uplifting and enlightening but I knew I'd be back and very soon. As the plane took off, I leant forward and gazed out of the window at the rapidly disappearing ground. As I sat back in my seat and clouds drifted past the plane's windows, my mind drifted back to how it all began, all those years ago in the outside loo.

Chapter Seventeen
The end for now

My hope is that you have enjoyed this work. If I have opened your eyes and encouraged some thoughts that we are not the only life registered on this earth of ours, then I have done my job. My hope is that I have in some way persuaded, or dare I suggest, convinced one person that, not only is there a life after this one, but that it is more than possible to communicate with our loved ones. My prayer is that through this book I have introduced you to an exciting way of life. It is not just for me, you also can open a doorway to many passageways. They are to be found within the heart; the key is in the mind.

Throughout my life I have been sandwiched between two worlds. It has been exciting, amazing, tender, thoughtful, scary, loving, satisfying, rewarding, comical, sad, honourable, pleasing, educating, breathtaking, heart stopping but never lonely. I have met people who are warm, kind, honest, caring, considerate, loving, truthful, tearful, happy, funny, honourable, thoughtful, pleasing, but never false. Most of my friends are from the spirit world. What are your friends like?

A long time ago, a gentleman stood in my living room. The vision did not instil fear within me. Instead he fired my soul to work long and hard for anyone who needed our help. Somewhere along the way in this life, I found the awakening. It would be a while before I agreed to act on this as my mind needed reasoning to function normally. I needed more than communicating with spirits, I needed positive results. I was, and still am, a hard master, refusing to take any old gibberish and call it mediumship. It was because of this steadfastness that highly evolved souls communicate through me today.

It was never my intention to be a medium. I would have preferred to be an artist or a singer. I do write, that is something I have enjoyed for many years.

Eventually a spirit helper encouraged me to write children's stories which I found I was able to produce in approximately forty minutes flat. All these works are gifts of the spirit. I will not ignore them. If they benefit someone, then my work is complete.

The spirit world has plans for me. When the time is right, I will know what I should do and where I should go next to help another on this long road we call life. I shall wait patiently until the time I hear that voice once again. You see, it's A Calling Of Angels.